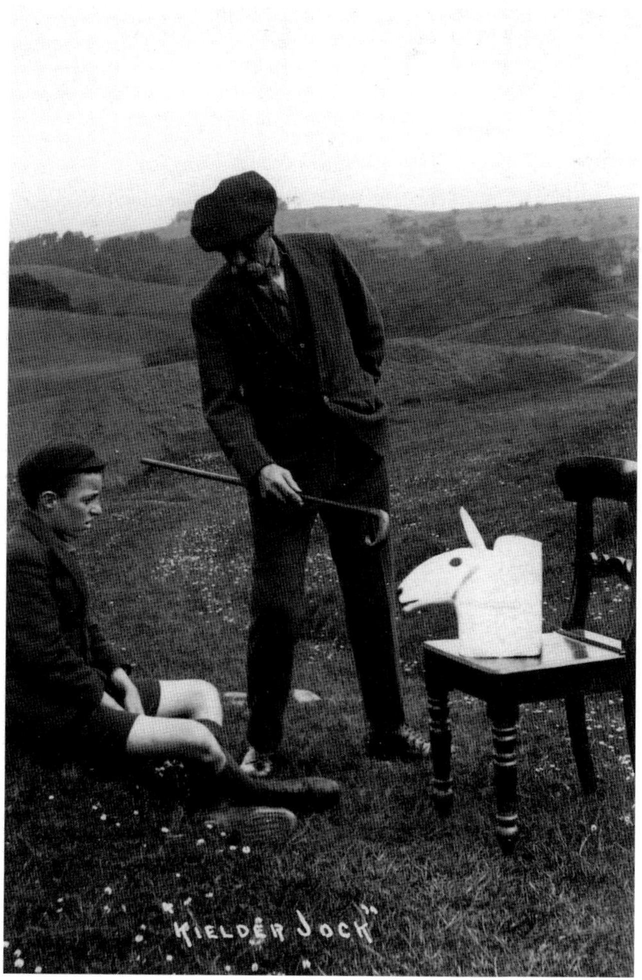


**John Davidson** a local character Collier and eve Jock. Here he i young James W of The Eals farm the finer p about Cheviot sheep, using one of the two wooden heads that he carved and kept in glass cabinets. Born on the remote farm of Kielder Head, John spent most of his life as a shepherd in the North Tyne Valley, except for fifteen years that he and his younger brother Oliver spent in America. Oliver stayed in America and worked in the movie industry but by 1892 John had returned to Plashetts and by 1901 was at Low Carriteth, the farm of his father and younger brother, Elliot Davidson (1864-1953). John had an unrivalled knowledge of Cheviot sheep and was regularly seen eyeing up stock at the local marts. A poet and noted fiddle-player, John Davidson, who spent his final years in Bellingham, is best known for the tune that he composed called Kielder Jock.

**ALLENDALE** was a centre of lead mining for 200 years but, as the falling price of lead and cheap foreign imports forced most of the mines to close towards the end of the 19th century, Allendale Town reinvented itself as an inland health resort. In the same year as the Allen Smelt Mill closed, the Newcastle Journal of 21st August 1896 recognised the increasing trend among the middle class to holiday in rural districts rather than at the seaside resorts and extolled the claims of Allendale as a desirable destination in the summer months. *The increase in the number of visitors during the past two years has been almost phenomenal and Allendale bids fair to become as famous as a health resort as in bygone years it was for its lead mining industry. The total and absolute extinction of the latter industry in recent years has reduced this once busy and thriving dale into a mere shadow of its former self. Large numbers of the hardy dalesmen have been obliged to quit the land of their home in quest of work elsewhere, thus severing, in form, but not in thought, that magical tie, which bound them to the heatherclad hills of their birth. The influx of visitors, therefore, has served in some measure to counteract the depressing influences created by the gradual depopulation of the dale and has produced a general liveliness and activity in the summer months unknown for many years.* Aided by the Hexham-Allendale railway until its closure to passengers on and from 22nd September 1930 and by bus firms eager for business, which, according to the Hexham Courant of 11th May 1929, made Allendale *the most be-bussed place in the kingdom for its importance and population,* Allendale fulfilled this function for almost a century. When Ethel Rood (1894-1986) retired aged 83 just before Christmas 1976 from the King's Head Hotel, where she had reigned for 50 years, she reminisced in the Hexham Courant of 21st January 1977 about the business or professional people from Newcastle and Tyneside, who came to the King's Head to re-charge themselves in the incomparable air of Allendale. *We were never done, cooking, baking, cleaning and putting bottles in the beds to keep them warm. The stage coach stopped every morning on its way from Allenheads. It would pick up people staying at the hotel to take them to the station to catch their trains to work.* Allendale station has become the Allendale Caravan Park. The days of Allendale as an inland health resort may have gone but Dale and Town still have much to offer visitors, walkers and those interested in industrial history and lead mining.

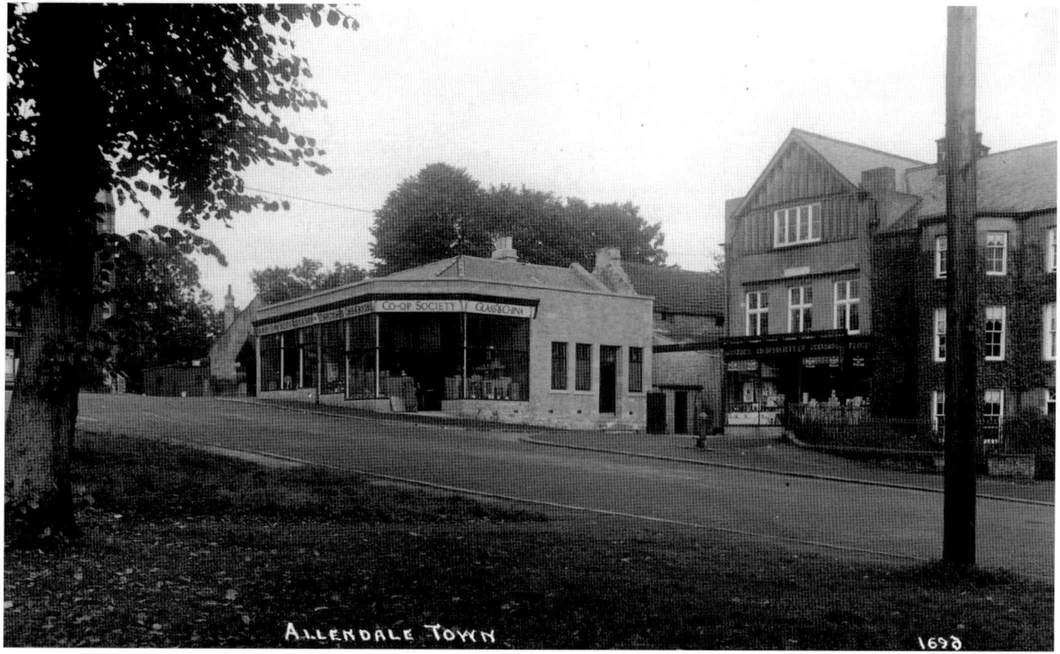


**ALLENDALE** Ten members, each contributing £5, founded the Allendale Industrial and Provident Co-operative Society in 1874. From its humble beginnings in a small building behind Forster's Temperance Hotel, which later became the wash-house of the Dale Hotel, the award-winning, independent Co-op has become the largest retailer in Allendale. This picture, one of the last of W. P. Collier, shows the new drapery, glass and furniture showroom, built on the site of West View, which opened on Saturday 13th June 1936 beside the grocery and hardware shop in Curtain House next door and the butchery in Shield Street. Curtain House closed when the whole business moved into the former showroom, which reopened on Wednesday 5th December 1990 as a modern supermarket, and the redundant premises were let to other retailers.

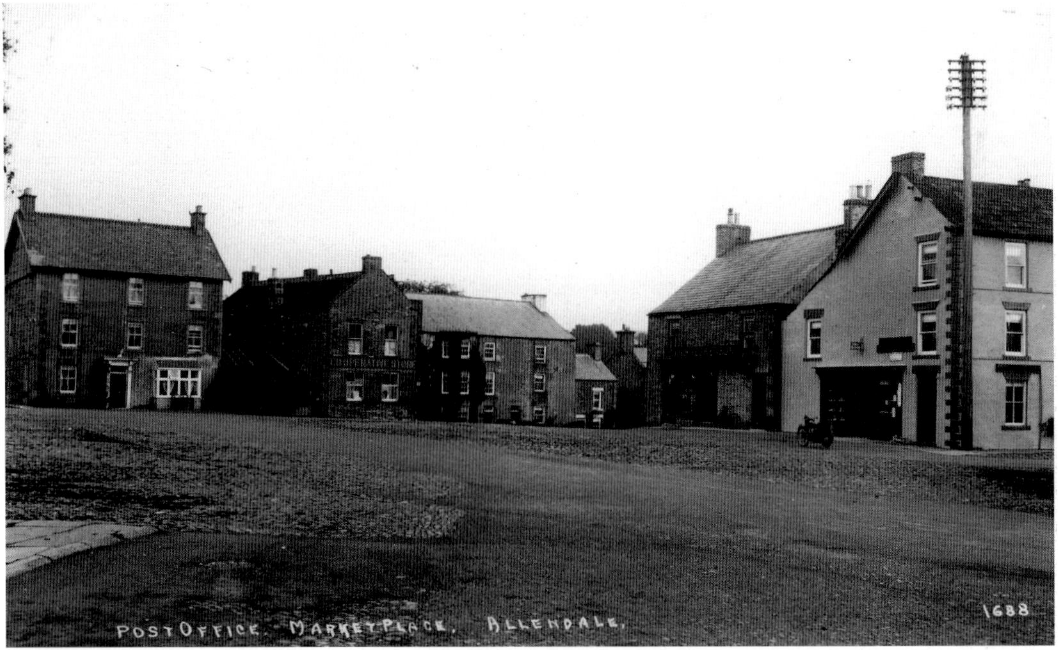


**ALLENDALE** The motorcycle of W. P. Collier stands outside the post office of Llewellyn Fairlamb (1876-1952), third son of William Fairlamb, who in 1899 had married Mary Hannah Bell, daughter of Lancelot and Jane Bell, proprietors of the Rose and Crown. The contents of the shop of John Ridley Stephenson (1858-1935), a grocer and provision dealer, were sold by auction on 6th June 1931. He was the eldest son of Matthew Stephenson and for several years was the proprietor of Allen House. This picture was taken shortly before West House, on the left, was demolished in favour of the new showroom of the Co-operative Society. West House was once the home of John James Allison (1845-1915), a Methodist preacher and chairman of the Parish Council, who had been the manager of the Co-operative Stores for 33 years.

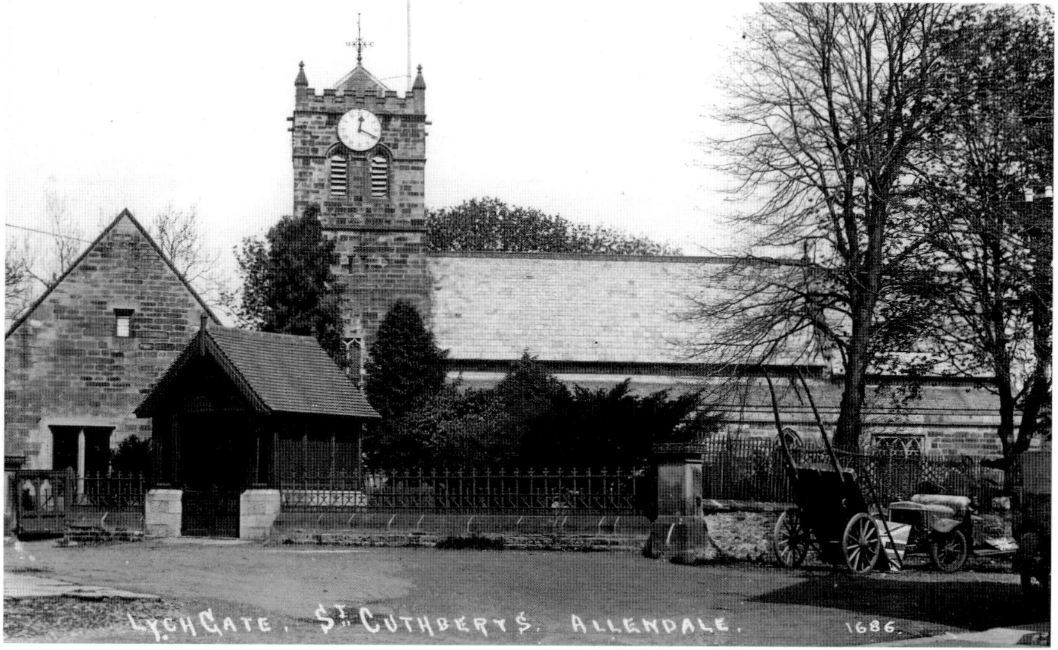


**ALLENDALE** The ancient parish church of St. Cuthbert was rebuilt in 1807 and restored in 1873-1874 by Austin and Johnson, at a cost of nearly £1,800, when the tower was raised about 15 feet. An 1842 sundial on the south wall cites the latitude of 54°50´ to state the claim of Allendale Town as the geographical centre of Britain. In front of the Sunday School, built in 1879, stands the imposing lych gate, which was unveiled by Viscountess Allendale on 14th August 1920 and records the names of the 22 men of Allendale who fell in the Great War. Two names were added after the Second World War. The stone flags of the floor were salvaged from the former Allen Smelt Mill. The church clock was erected in 1906 in memory of the Chatt family of Moor Houses at a cost of £140, each of its three faces being 5ft 6in in diameter.

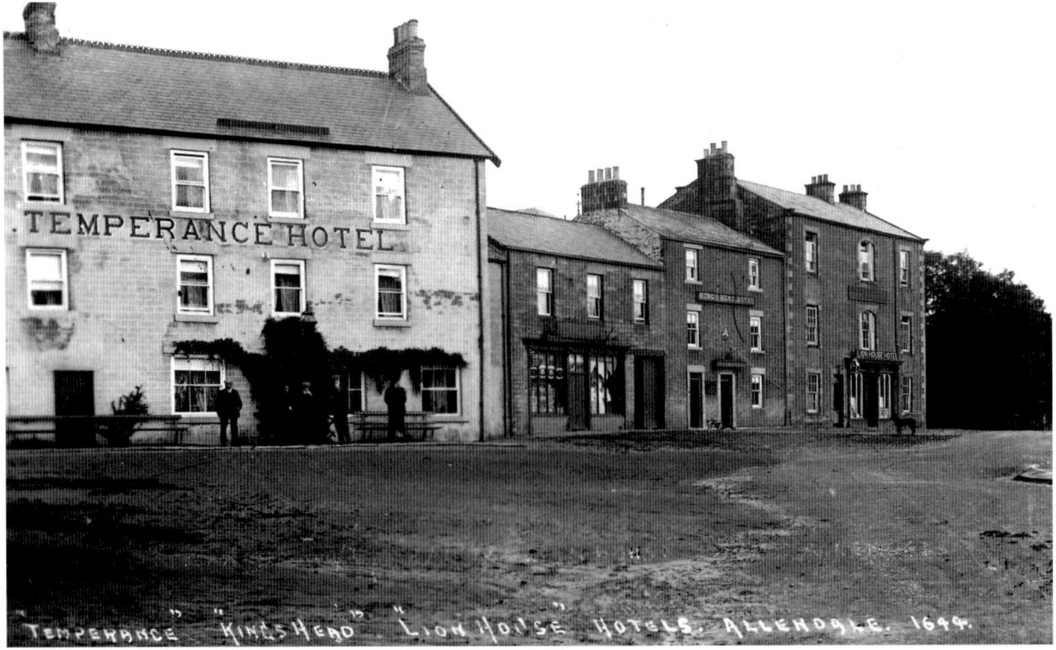


**ALLENDALE** This inland resort had a ready market for postcards because many hotels and boarding houses catered for visitors in search of health, change of air, or scene. Three hotels dominate the Market Place. For forty years, the Temperance Hotel was run by Joseph and Mary Forster, then daughters Isabella & Mary Jane Forster, until it passed to the Simpson family in May 1920. The shop of Herbert Edgar (1864-1934), draper and grocer, was built by his father David Edgar in 1863 on the site of the Three Tuns Inn, separating the Temperance Hotel and the King's Head Hotel and Lion House Hotel, now the Golden Lion. In 1926, Ethel May Rood (1894-1986) with her husband George (1893-1956) took over the King's Head from her mother, Elizabeth Mary West, and ran the hotel for fifty years until her retirement at Christmas 1976.

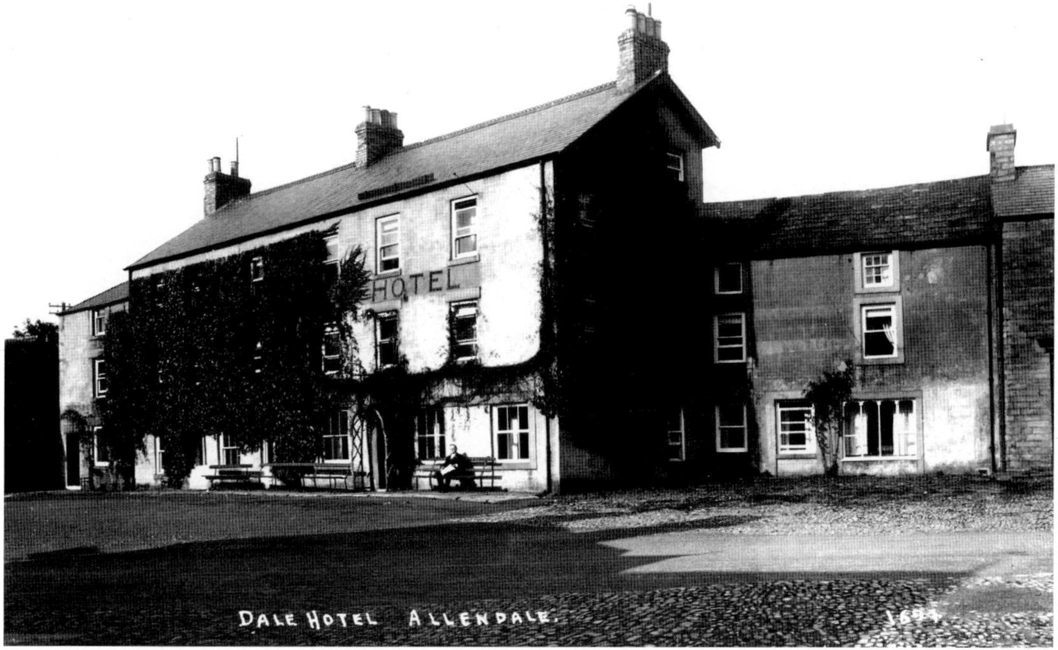


**ALLENDALE** William and Margaret Simpson took over the Temperance Hotel in May 1920 and changed its name to the Dale Hotel. Their daughter Mary Constance (1893-1974) ran the hotel after her marriage to George Arcus Thompson in 1927 and their only son William Arcus Thompson (1929-2000) continued with his wife Rita (1932-1996) after the retirement of his mother. *The Temperance Hotel can claim to have been the pioneer not so much in meeting a demand for boarding house accommodation but in creating it. The first visitors to Allendale stayed at the Temperance, mainly South Shields and Sunderland folks. They went back home to speak well of it. More and more came, still chiefly from Shields and Sunderland. Newcastle then discovered Allendale as a health and holiday resort.* (Hexham Courant 17th April 1920)

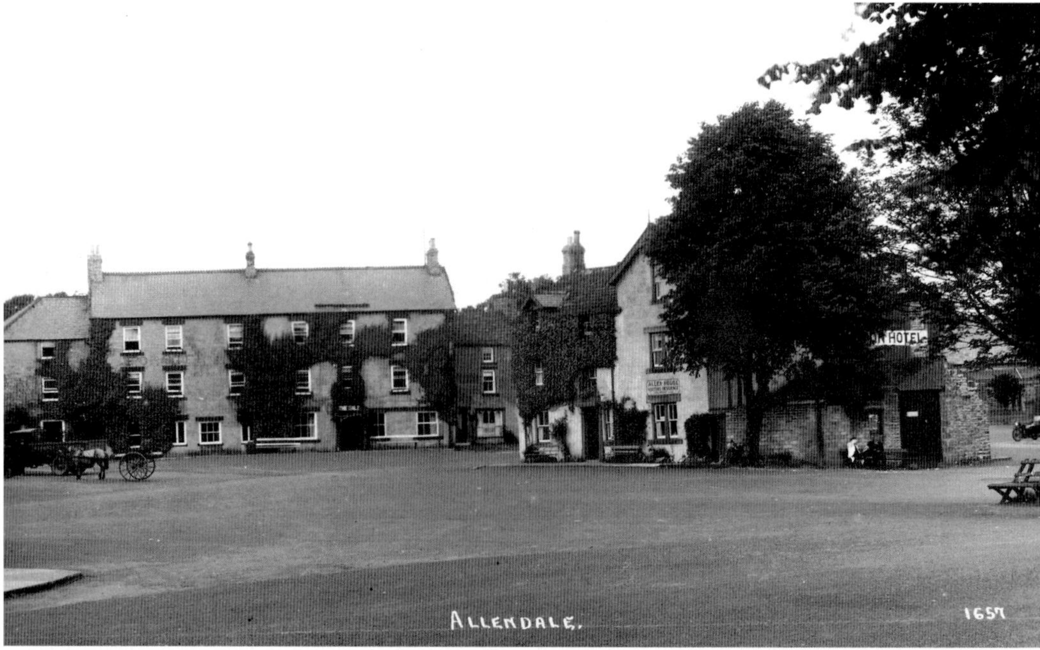


**ALLENDALE** The title of Forster's Temperance Hotel is still visible some years after it was renamed the Dale Hotel. A plaque was unveiled on its east wall on 5th July 1997 to mark 250 years of Methodism begun in July 1747 by Christopher Hopper (1722-1802), who was one of the earliest travelling preachers of John Wesley. There was a strong Temperance tradition among the lead miners and Allendale was a favourite venue for Temperance meetings, which were held in the field near the Temperance Hall and included a band, speeches, sports and tea. Excursion trains brought members from other temperance branches. A lorry and horse and cart stand outside the smithy of William Hutchinson between the Dale Hotel and Heatherlea, each able to accommodate 60 or 70 guests. Allen House on the right was a smaller boarding house.

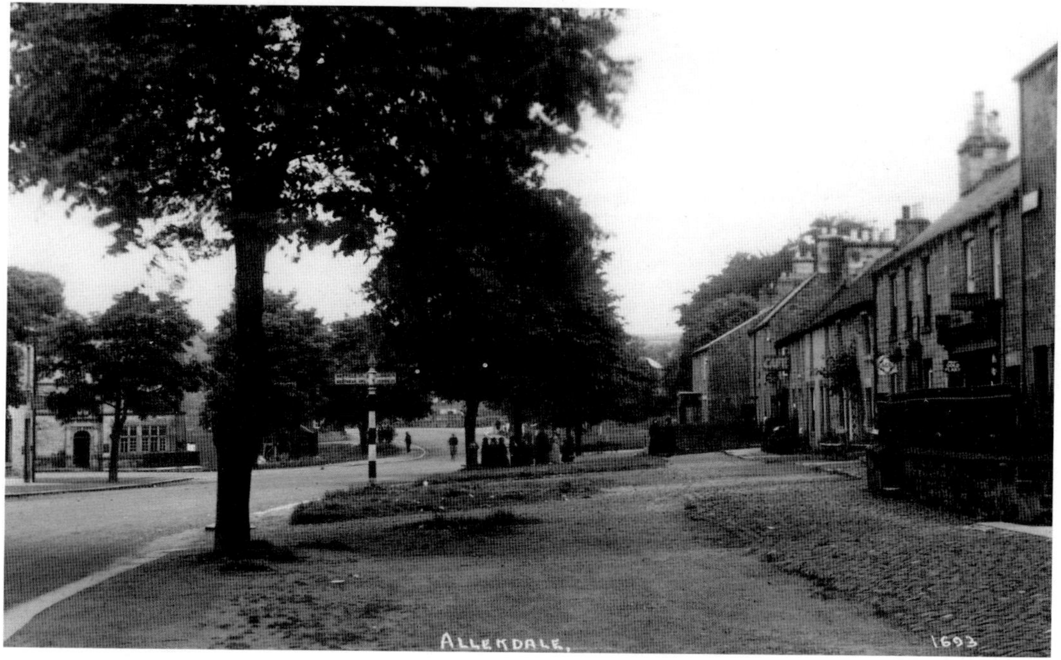


**ALLENDALE** Arnison Terrace was named after George Arnison (1830-1904), for 50 years local surgeon and benefactor. People stand outside the bakery and café of George Dick (1893-1978), possibly waiting for their coach. Other shops in this terrace included the confectionery shop of Cissie Dodd, nearest the camera, next door to which was the Rose and Crown Inn. This old hostelry was never the same after the death on 25th March 1921 of Jane Bell, aged 75, for nearly 35 years its respected hostess, whose husband Lancelot had died in 1892. After being sold on 8th February 1927, it had become by 1932 Ye Olde Oaks tearooms and then a boarding house. It opened for a year as a Youth Hostel at Easter 1936. It continued as a café and guest house until it became between 1964 and 1989 the home of sculptor Charles Sansbury.

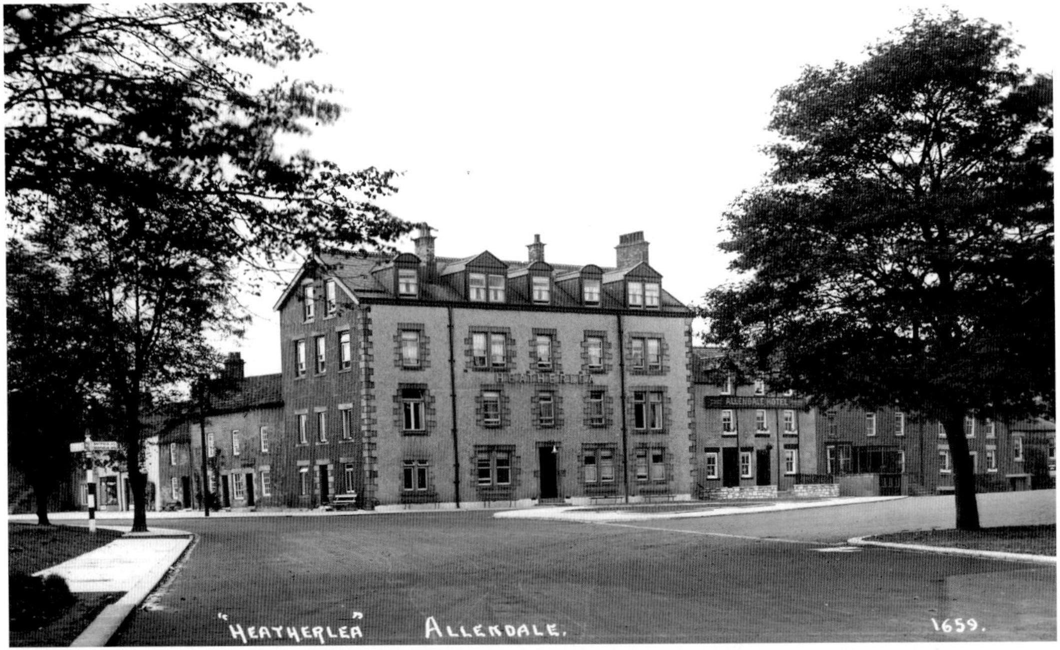


**HEATHERLEA** Matthew Stephenson (1832-1907) and his son-in-law George Bell (1866-1934) converted a two-storey building, which housed the shop of Matthew Stevenson, grocer & draper, and branch manager of the Cumberland Union Bank, into a four-storey temperance hotel. The Heatherlea opened in 1901 and for over ninety years was one of the most popular hotels in Allendale with a loyal clientele, who would sit on the benches outside. After the death of resident proprietor George Bell, the hotel passed in turn to George and Mabel Parkinson, Joseph and Mary Parker, Margaret (née Parker) and Thomas Shield and John and Helen Shield. Falling numbers of visitors in the 1990s prompted the development of the hotel as a restaurant and then its conversion into three spacious apartments, which were let from February 2000.

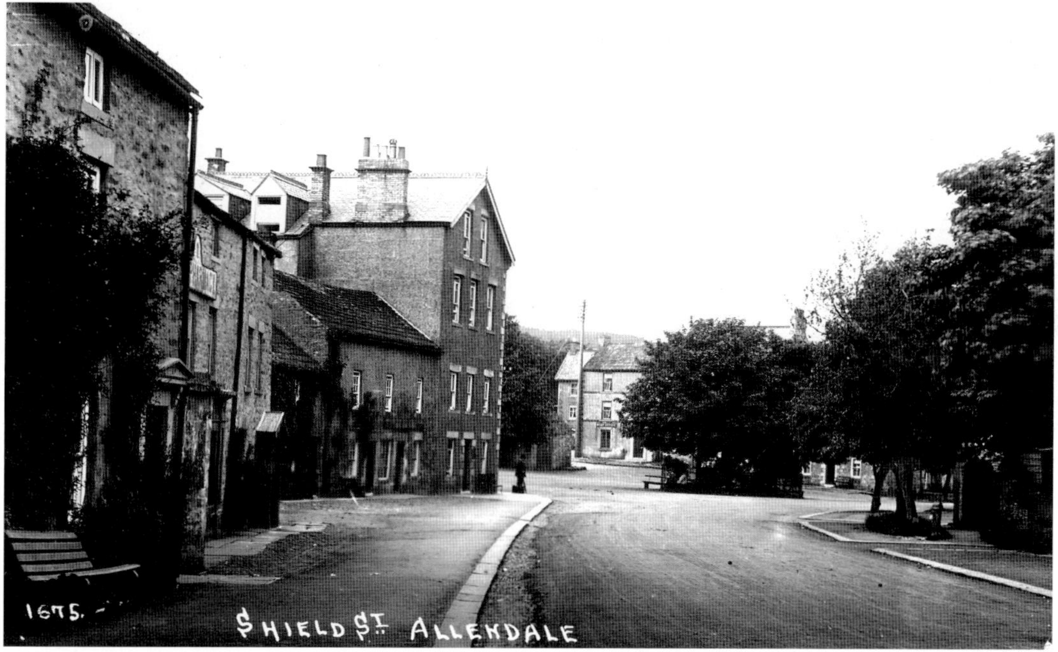


**SHIELD STREET** On the left is the pharmacy of Henry Blake, who sold medicines, toilet preparations and photographic supplies. The three modern houses next door were built in 1984 after fire destroyed the shop, café and home of the Tulip family on 3rd October 1977. Facing the trees of the bull ring is the Heatherlea Hotel, which stood opposite Hotspur House, hidden by trees on the right. To the left of the telegraph pole is a corner of West House, dating this picture prior to 1936, when the new Co-op opened on its site. To the right of the pole is the post office of three generations of the Fairlamb family, who served Allendale as postmasters for almost 100 years: William Fairlamb (1871-1904), Llewellyn Fairlamb (1904-1951) and William Redvers Fairlamb (1951-1970), who in 1953 moved the post office next door to its present location.

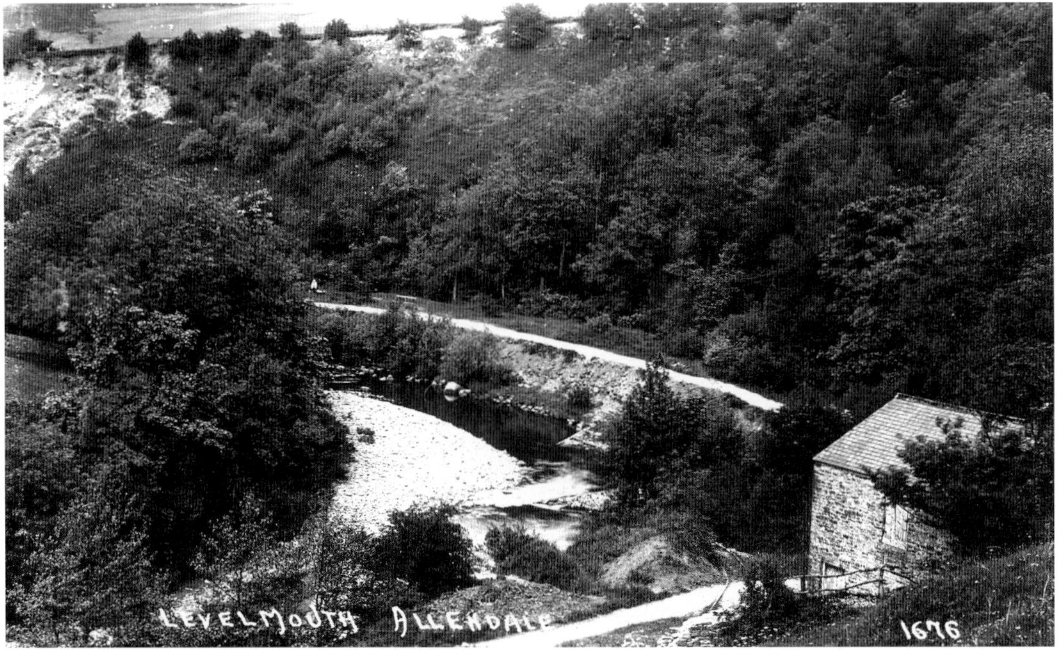


**BLACKETT LEVEL** Lead mining had all but gone when W. P. Collier took this picture of the most ambitious undertaking of Thomas Sopwith (1803-1879), who was the Chief Agent for the Blackett-Beaumont mines from 1845 to 1871. The Blackett Level was a tunnel, designed to be almost seven miles long and with a gradient of nine feet per mile, which was driven beside the building on the right to find new veins of lead and drain the mine at Allenheads. It was started in 1854 but never finished because the market for lead crashed in 1878. The best quality and most easily accessible ores had gone and it was cheaper to import ore from Spain and other countries. Thomas Sopwith provided schools, libraries, lectures and social benefits for the Allendale miners and is known today as the man who changed the face of the Dale.

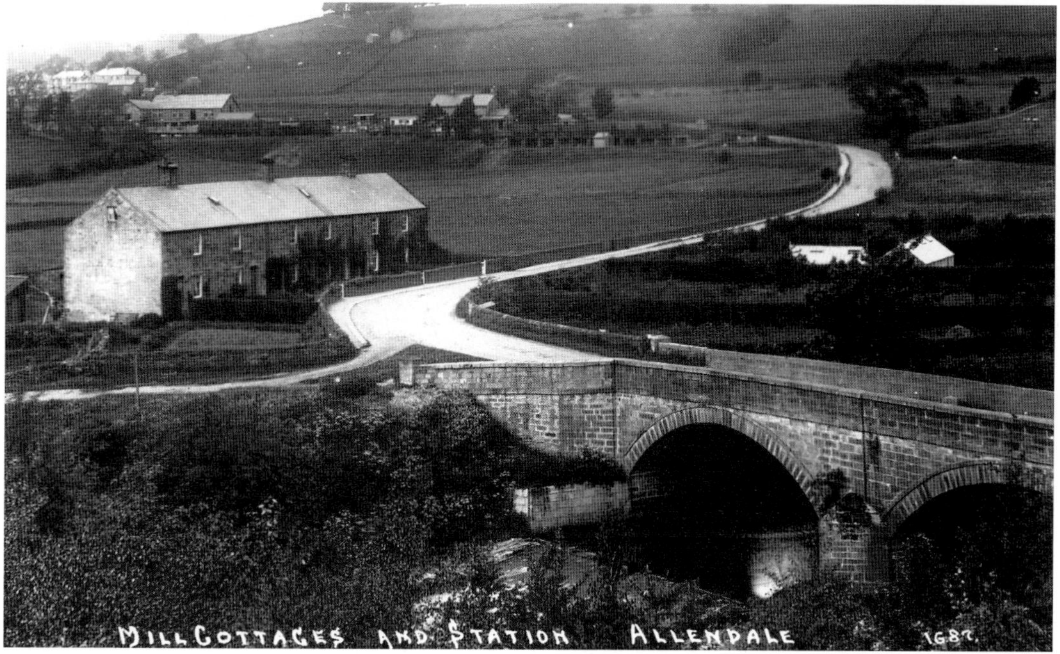


**MILL COTTAGES** Between Mill Cottages and the village of Catton stands Catton Road station, renamed Allendale in May 1898 to stamp the claim of Allendale as a holiday resort. A siding ran to the adjacent Allen Smelt Mill. The Hexham to Allendale line opened to passengers on 1st March 1869 but a lack of capital meant that the line never ran beyond Catton Road, over a mile from Allendale Town. The regular service on the single-track line in the 1920s was three trains each way while over thirty buses served Allendale Town every day except Sundays. Excursion trains and Bank Holidays failed to limit losses and the last passenger train ran on 21st September 1930, an event that *passed with practically no attention.* The line kept open for goods traffic and a few excursions but the last goods train ran on 17th November 1950.

**MATFEN** was one of the favourite villages of W. W. Tomlinson, who wrote in his Comprehensive Guide to Northumberland (1888) *This charming little village, from its sheltered position and sweet rural attractions, bids fair to become a favourite resort of the dwellers of our large towns in need of rest and quiet. It is agreeably remote from the sound of the railway whistle and still retains some of the old Arcadian peace and simplicity.* The township of West Matfen had existed for generations but the estate village of Matfen was largely the creation of Sir Edward Blackett (1805-1885), who succeeded to the Matfen Estate on the death of his father Sir William Blackett in 1816. He rebuilt Matfen Hall between 1832 and 1836. He built, at his sole expense, the church of Holy Trinity in 1842 and in 1854 added an imposing spire that the latest edition of The Buildings of England describes as *quite powerful with its very high broach spire*. To the north of the church arose the 19th century estate village of Matfen, including a school built by Sir Edward Blackett in 1845. Two lines of houses, North and South Side, face the village green, bisected by a water course, the creation of the Whittle Dean Water Company, which from 1863 became the Newcastle and Gateshead Water Company, to bring water from Colt Crag and Hallington to the reservoirs at Whittle Dean. The Black Bull did a roaring trade from the navvies, who lived in huts near Matfen, while engaged on the ambitious scheme of tunnels and aqueducts. Local tradition relates that around 1875 Sir Edward, increasingly concerned about the evils of drink, built the Blackett Arms Temperance Hotel, which he strategically located next to the Black Bull. The old Temperance Hotel, still proudly bearing the Blackett coat of arms, is now the Matfen Estates Office. As Bill (A. W.) Purdue wrote (2004) in his book, The Ship that Came Home, *The improvements of Sir Edward Blackett at Matfen were an expression of a social vision, shared by many of his contemporary landowners, of a harmonious, if layered, society, where the big house and church presided over prosperous farmers and a contented agricultural workforce. This strong vein of paternalism resulted in a considerable improvement in rural housing in Northumberland, as the very basic, heather-thatched cottages, common early in the 19th century, gave way to model villages with roomier and solidly built houses with gardens and with common social facilities, including reading rooms and village halls.* If you seek a monument to a Victorian visionary, look no further than Matfen!

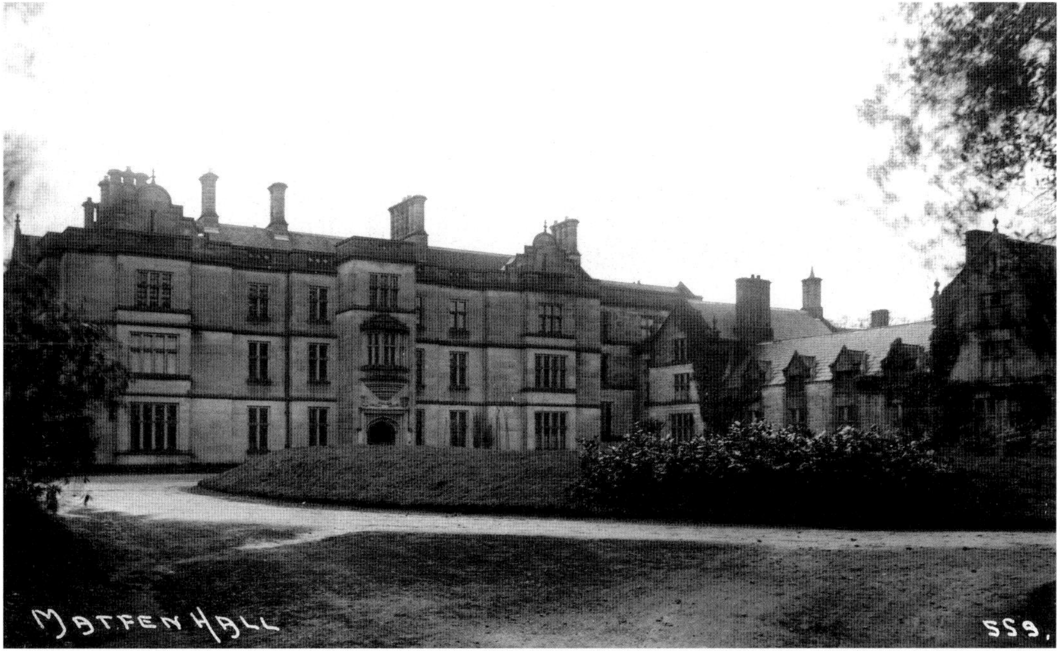


**MATFEN** A drive leads past Holy Trinity church to the north entrance to Matfen Hall, which overlooks the River Pont to the south and the modern 18-hole golf course. The Hall was built between 1832 and 1836 by Thomas Rickman for Sir Edward Blackett (1805-1885), who had inherited the Matfen Estate on the death of his father Sir William Blackett (1759-1816). He was succeeded by his son, Sir Edward William Blackett (1831-1909), and his grandson, Sir Hugh Douglas Blackett (1873-1960). Matfen Hall opened on 12th January 1967 as a Leonard Cheshire nursing home and closed on 31st October 1994 after moving to purpose-built facilities in Newcastle. A subsequent £2 million restoration saw Sir Hugh and Lady Anna Blackett open Matfen Hall in April 1999 as a luxurious and ultimately award-winning country hotel.

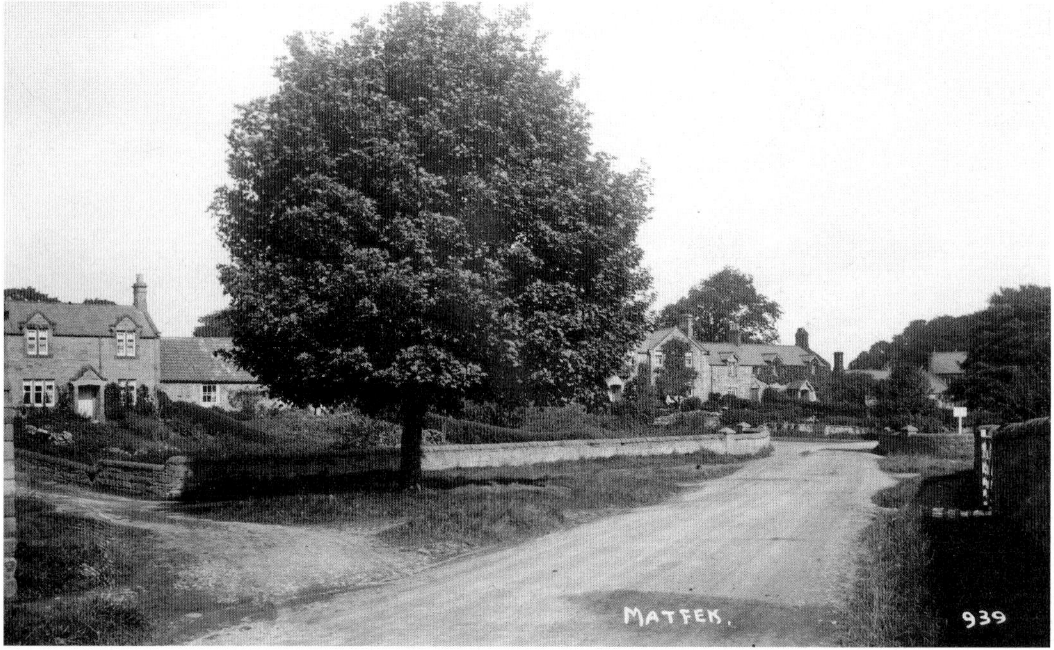


**MATFEN** This view looks east along the village, two miles north of the Military Road and approached by a drive from Matfen Piers, two stone gateposts standing on the line of the Roman Wall. Matfen is the 19th century estate village of Sir Edward Blackett (1805-1885), who lived in the village that he had built for nearly 50 years. North and South Side face each other across the village green. This picture shows the houses of North Side, with the house on the extreme left carrying the dedication A. & E. B. 1881: Alethea was the fourth and last wife of Sir Edward Blackett. The cottage next door became two-storey around 1963. Beyond the tree, removed in 2004, the road on the left leads to Ryal past the old Wesleyan Chapel, dating from 1840. At the eastern end of North Side were the former joinery, smithy and Temperance Hotel.

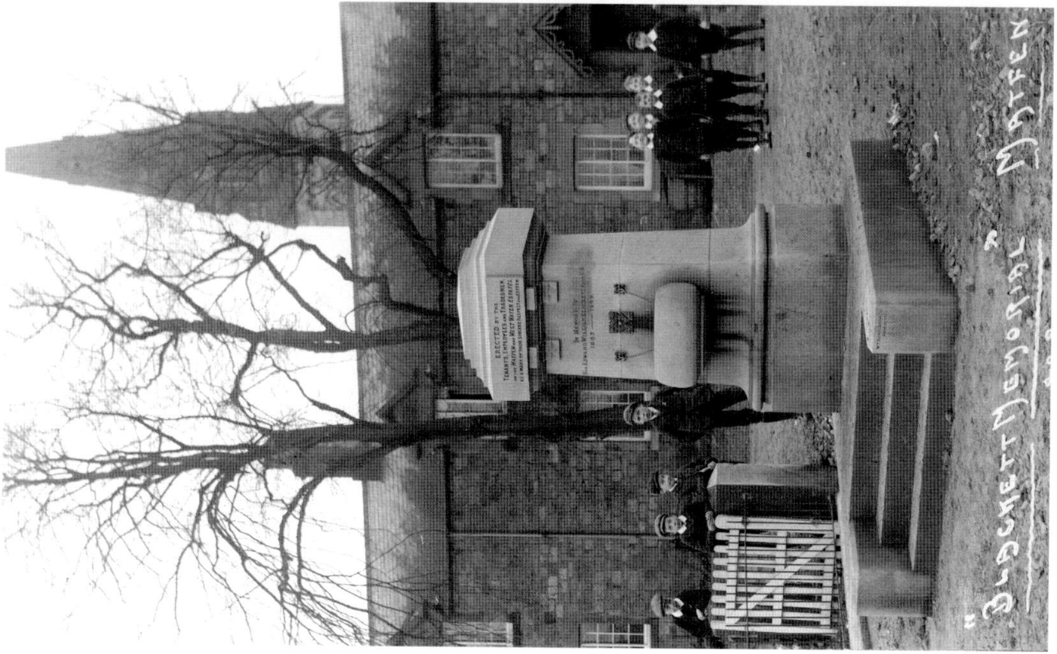


**MATFEN** Major-General Sir Edward William Blackett, C.B., of the Rifle Brigade and 7th Baronet of Matfen, died in London on 13th September 1909, aged 78 years, and his body was brought to Corbridge by rail, and thence to Matfen, for a simple interment on 18th September in the church of Holy Trinity that his father, Sir Edward Blackett, 6th Baronet, had built. In his memory, the tenants, employees and tradesmen on the Matfen and West Water estates erected a drinking fountain, which was dedicated on 12th November 1910. The fountain was designed by William Donaldson, a sculptor of Newcastle, and was built of Heworth stone, with a stone basin and drinking cups. The pipes and bronze fittings were supplied by the Newcastle and Gateshead Water Company, whose main feeder streams crossed several miles of the Matfen Estate.

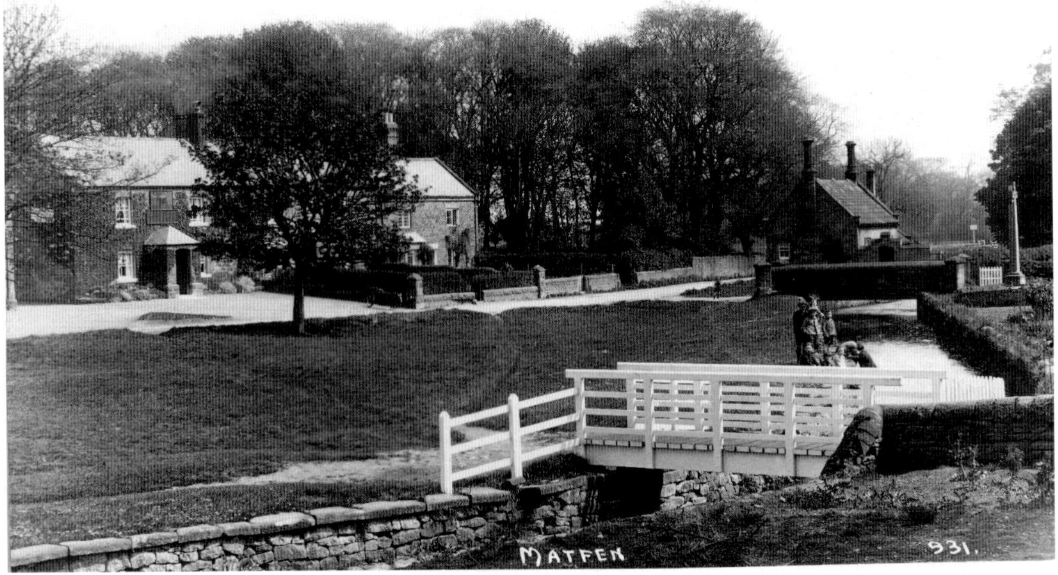


**MATFEN** The response of the Whittle Dean Water Company to the increasing demands of industrial Tyneside for supplies of fresh water was to impound the original group of five reservoirs at Whittle Dean, inaugurated in September 1848, with water from the upland districts lying to the west of Ryal via a series of aqueducts and a 3,887-yard tunnel at Ryal, which was completed by 31st December 1859. In August 1859, at the request of Sir Edward Blackett, an additional channel was formed to carry the water from the eastern end of the tunnel to Burnside without using the River Pont, which passed through the grounds of Matfen Hall. The result, much to the delight of the local children on this picture, was the feeder stream, or cut, that flows gently through Matfen and provides the final touch to the picturesque quality of the village.

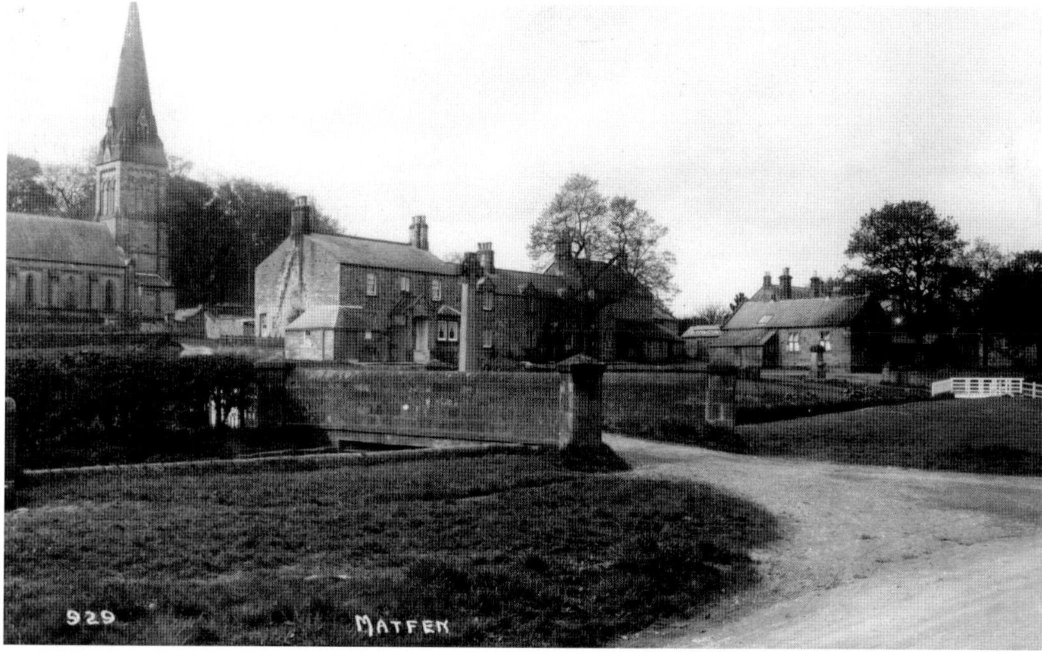


**MATFEN** This view from the School House looks across Church Road Bridge and the War Memorial towards the Blackett Memorial and school. The houses of East Close, completed in 1980 on former allotments, stand to the left of Holy Trinity Church and to the right are the houses of South Side and their well-tended gardens. Unveiled on Saturday 1st May 1920, the War Memorial takes the form of a Celtic cross and has the names of the 22 local men who died in the First World War. The Role of Honour in the church lists the names of the 84 men who served. Three names were added after the Second World War. On the far left is Matfen School, built by Sir Edward Blackett in 1845, which closed to its seven pupils on 21st July 1972 when Nancy Murray was headteacher. It now houses the enterprising village store and coffee shop.

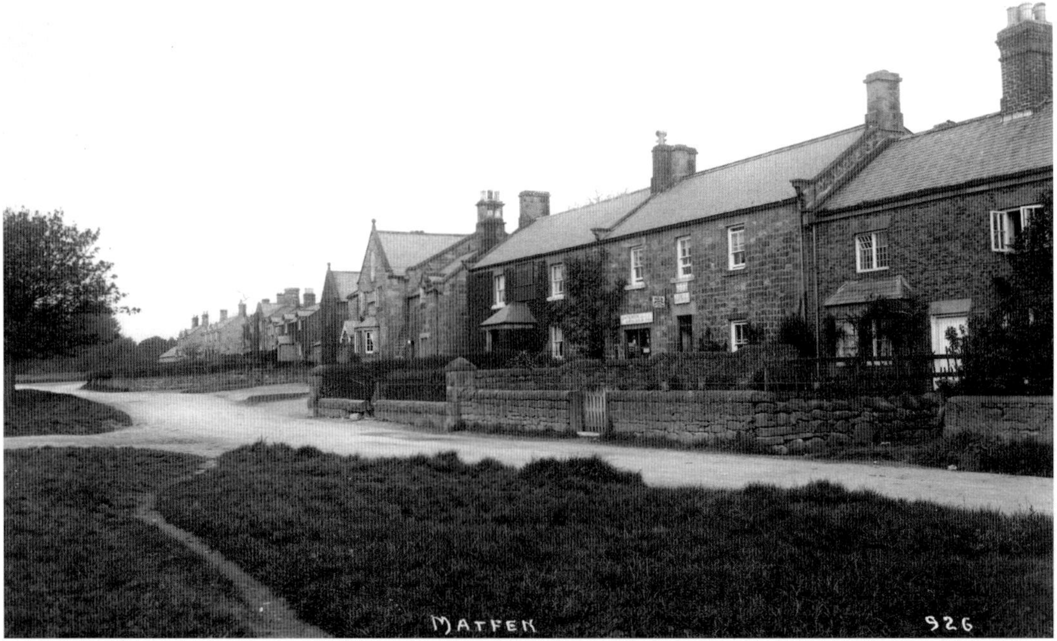


**MATFEN** To the left of the School House stands Rose Cottage, which carries the name of Jacob Atkinson (1863-1950), who became postmaster on the death in 1920 of his wife Isabella, postmistress for 12 years. The Black Bull Inn, hosted for over 25 years by Thomas Black (1862-1921) and then by Rebecca Milburn, his stepdaughter, is still the village local. The Blackett Arms Hotel was built to support the Temperance Movement and is now the Matfen Estates Office. Alma House was the home of James Thomas (Tot) Robson (1896-1977), a joiner and Methodist preacher, the son of joiner and cartwright Thomas Brown Robson (1863-1944) and the grandson of joiner Thomas Robson (1825-1889), both of whom ran the Temperance Hotel in the 1880s and 1890s after the untimely death of proprietor George Cowle (1830-1882).

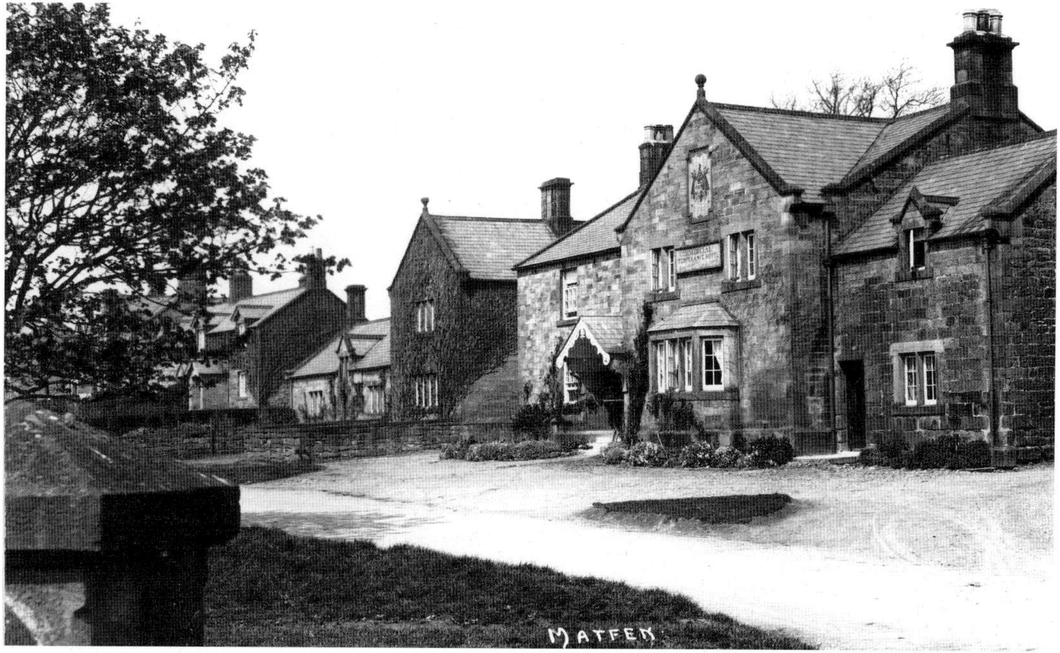


**MATFEN** Margaret (1859-1931) and Thomas (1861-1937) Leathard ran the Temperance Hotel until 30th May 1931, and then James (1867-1940) and Jane (1886-1949) Beattie. On her death, her daughter Dorothy (1919-2004) and husband Ronald Dutton (1918-1983) ran the hotel, which was famous for the food cooked by Dorothy Dutton, a reserved and helpful lady, who did teas for cycling clubs. She still provided accommodation for her regular guests after the death of her husband. After she moved to Blackett Cottages, which opened on 6th October 1994, the hotel became a house and from 2000 the Matfen Estates Office. The double-storey building is Forge House, where Thomas Armstrong (1900-1972), the last blacksmith, lived from 1929 until his death. The single-storey building was the Forge, which became a house in 1980.

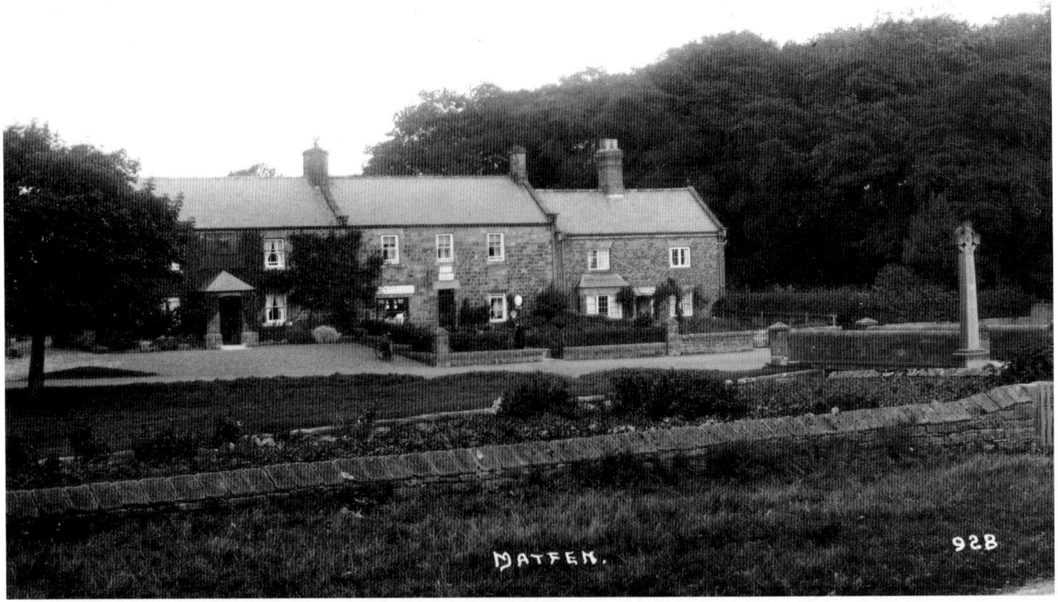


**MATFEN** Parking his motorcycle outside the Black Bull, W. P. Collier has taken this view of the post office and *Anything and Everything* shop of Jacob Atkinson, which now sports a petrol pump. After his retirement in 1935, the post office moved into the shop behind the Temperance Hotel and Rose Cottage became a sweet shop, which spinsters Edith Maud Black (1888-1973) and her stepsister Rebecca Dewbury Milburn (1883-1962) ran into the late 1950s. The shop had jars of sweets on the shelves but was dark and rather intimidating. Miss Black was old-fashioned and wore her hair in a bun with plaits coiled on each side. She sold black bullets in cone-shaped bags and would cut a sweet in half to get the right weight. After spells as a house and restaurant of the Black Bull, the old shop reverted to a private residence in September 2001.

**SIMONBURN** exudes a tangible air of tranquillity that belies its military and ecclesiastical importance in medieval times. Simonburn Castle dates from the 13th century but was demolished in the 18th century by local people in a vain search for buried treasure. The Church of St. Mungo also dates from the 13th century, with the first recorded Rector of 1229 being Master Mathew, Archdeacon of Cleveland, who rebuilt the chancel. Most of the present structure dates from a series of refurbishments in the 18th and 19th centuries. Earlier Rectors had a pele tower for protection but the Reverend Major Allgood (1637-1696) built a new rectory, when he became Rector in 1666, with the present Georgian frontage being added in 1725. The tower was demolished in 1832 to repair the garden walls. Much of the village of Simonburn dates from the time when Sir Lancelot Allgood (1710-1782) built Nunwick Hall between 1746 and 1750 and removed the existing village of Nunwick to Simonburn, where he built houses for workers on the Nunwick Estate. John Wallis, Curate of Simonburn, found the sylvan surroundings conducive to his writing of The Natural History and Antiquities of Northumberland (1769), even if his relationship with his Rector, James Scott, was stormy. Wallis praised Sir Lancelot Allgood, who had *given a new face, as it were, to the country about Nunwick, within the space of a very few years, by making plantations, enclosures, and good roads, one of which leads to the village of Simonburn.* He is said to have written much of his work while sitting on the banks of the Tecket Linn, which itself teems with flora and fauna, details of which he carefully included in the first volume. William Hutchinson, in his View of Northumberland (1776), found *little that is remarkable to detain the traveller* other than that Simonburn was (until 1818) *the largest parish in the diocese, extending northward from Chollerford Bridge to Liddesdale in Scotland, a space of 32 measured miles.* Lancelot John Hunter Allgood (1823-1885) succeeded to the Nunwick Estate in 1854 and Bulmer, in his History and Directory of Northumberland (1886), noted that Simonburn had been *greatly improved of late years, several of the dilapidated cottages having been replaced by tasteful and well-built residences.* Simonburn lost the Red Lion Inn around 1875 and its coal mine at Goatstones in 1932. The village shop and post office provides a tea room, craft shop and bed and breakfast. Simonburn remains a peaceful village at the heart of the Nunwick Estate and maintains a charm that is rare and timeless.

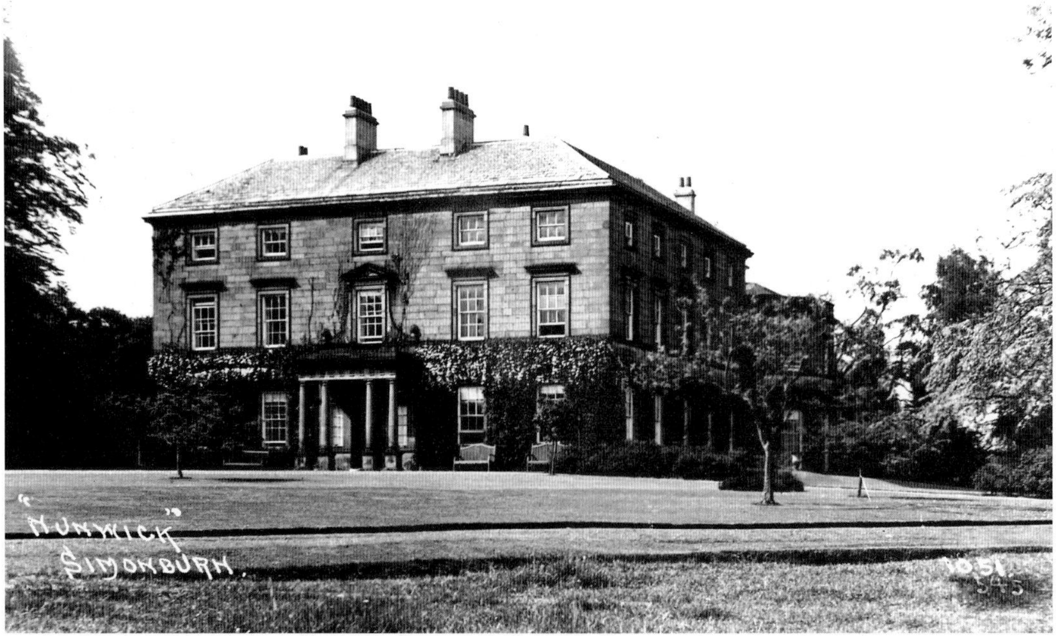


**NUNWICK** The private residence of Nunwick Hall stands in a beautifully wooded park, half a mile east of Simonburn. Nunwick itself was once a village with its own manor house and village green but in 1724 the manor of Simonburn was sold by Sir Harry Heron of Chipchase to Robert Allgood, whose only daughter and heir married Lancelot Allgood, who was knighted in 1760. He swept everything away except for a few trees and between 1746 and 1750 had a new hall built on the site of the old manor house. The main block of Nunwick consists of five bays, facing south and east, and is one of the finest designs of Daniel Garrett, who created Wallington Hall. Ignatius Bonomi added the striking four-column Doric porch in 1829. The gardens of Nunwick, famous for its hostas, are opened once a year in aid of the Red Cross.

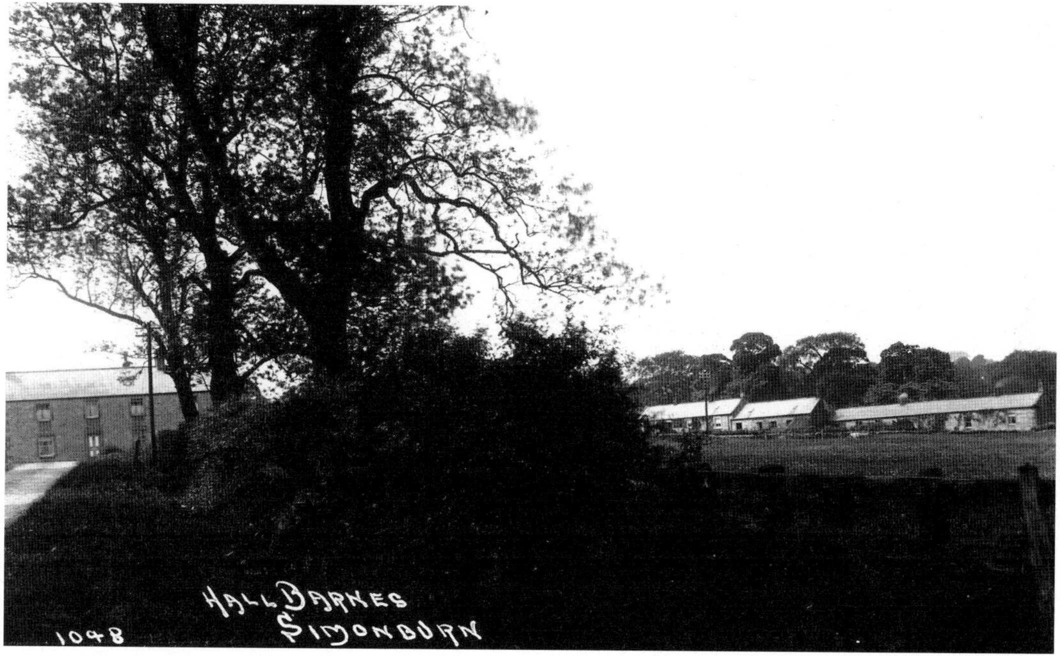


**HALL BARNS** On the far left of the terrace of cottages was the house and smithy of Francis Boyd (1845-1918). On the death of his father, Francis H. Boyd (1878-1957) became blacksmith. Horses could often be seen queuing up outside his smithy waiting to be shod while beads of sweat would be running down the forehead of this master craftsman, who was a careful worker and would take his time to shoe a horse. He was a gentle man but very strong and was used to shoeing heavy farm horses and repairing farm machinery. He had three fields and a few cows and sold milk in the locality. Eric Liddle started as an apprentice to Francis Boyd on the day after he left Simonburn School at the age of fourteen. He took over the forge when he was in his early twenties and retired after 56 years' service in November 1997 on his 70th birthday.

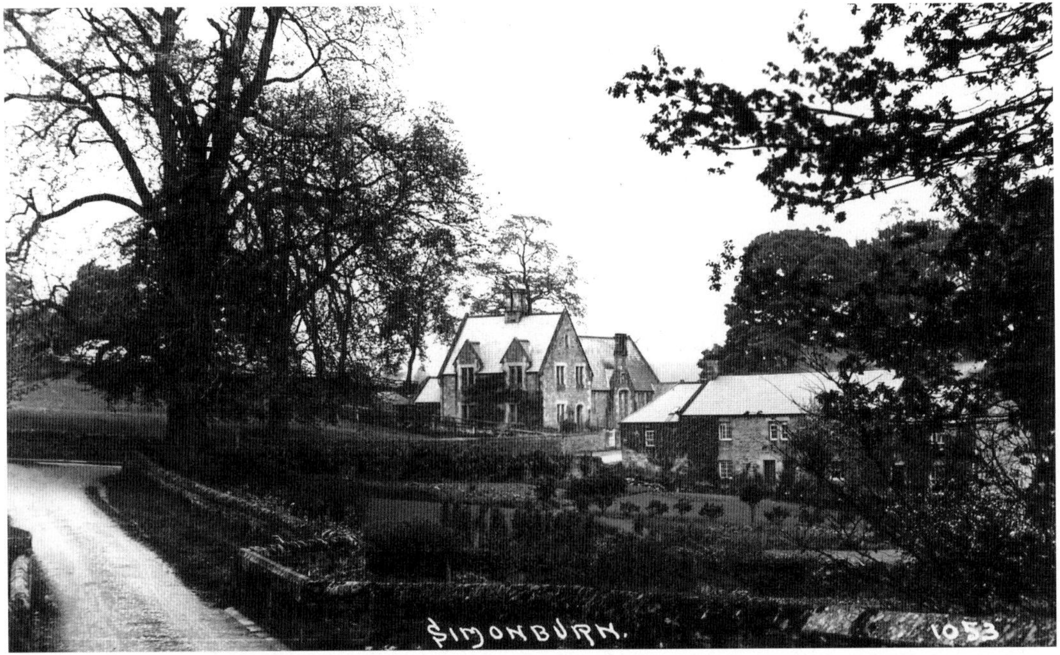


**SIMONBURN** Descending sharply from Hall Barns, the road crosses a small bridge built in 1708 over the Crook Burn and turns left into Simonburn. Opposite Bridge View Cottages, on the right, stand the new school house and school for 50 pupils, which Lancelot John Hunter Allgood conveyed to the Rector and Churchwardens of Simonburn on 23rd November 1857. The premises were later improved for public meetings and for the Simonburn Reading Room and Parish Library, whose 30 members shared about 400 volumes. The school closed quietly on 10th April 1965 and the pupils began the summer term on 27th April at the new Wark Church of England Primary School, which was officially opened on 9th July 1965. The Nunwick Estate duly allowed the former school premises to be converted into Simonburn village hall.

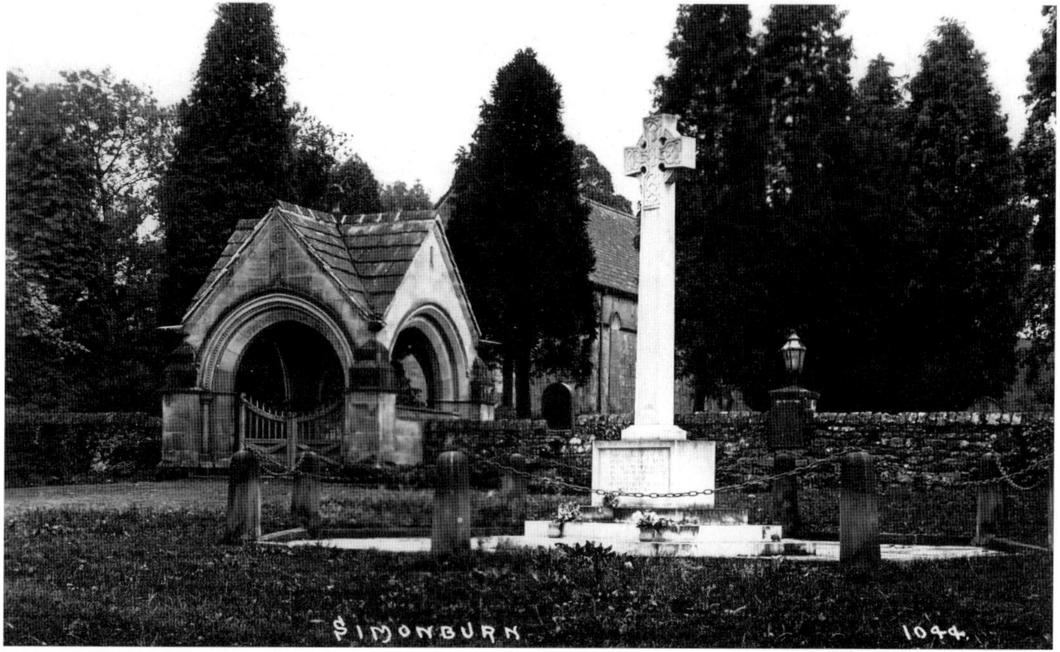


**SIMONBURN** Little survives of the original 13th century church of St. Mungo, which was, until 1818, the mother church of the Great Parish of Simonburn that stretched from the Roman Wall to Carter Bar. The importance of the building is matched by the grandeur of the lych gate, designed by W. S. Hicks of Newcastle and built by W. Wilson of Gilsland. Erected in memory of Lancelot John Hunter Allgood (1823-1885) by his family, friends and tenants, it was dedicated on Sunday 2nd May 1886. He succeeded to the Nunwick Estate in 1854 on the death of his father, Robert Lancelot Allgood. Highly respected and deeply interested in Estate matters, he built Simonburn School and replaced several of the older cottages. The War Memorial was unveiled on Sunday 30th May 1920 by Brigadier-General W. H. L. Allgood, C.M.G., D.S.O.

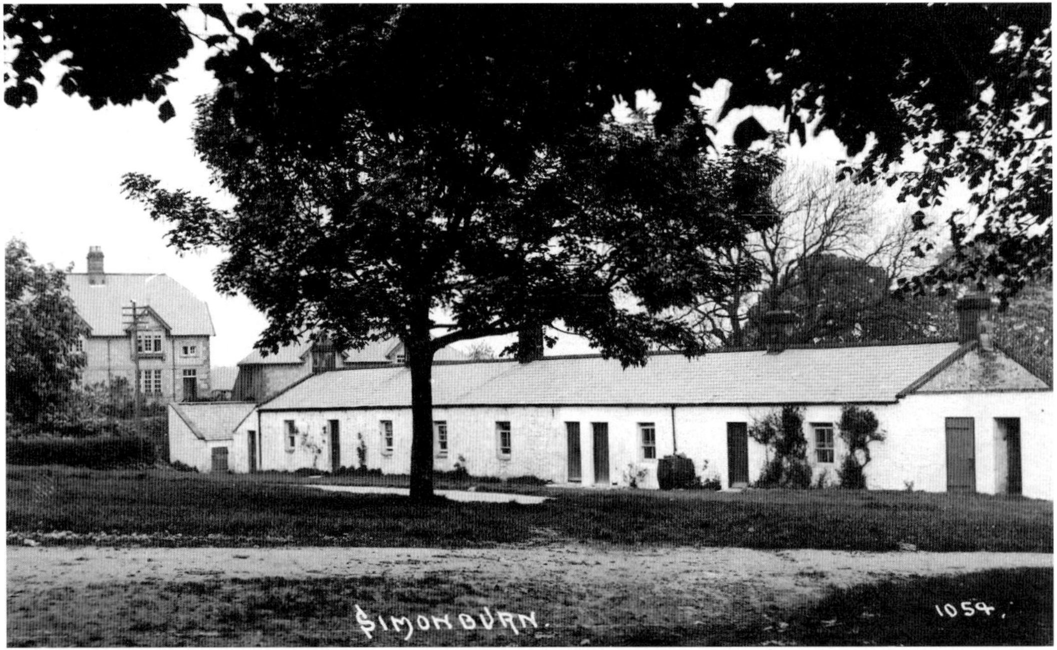


**SIMONBURN** This picture shows the original four cottages of The Green, which were built for the Nunwick Estate workers under the direction of the Steward, who had a large house to the rear. The cottage on the right once served the purpose of a school but, on the opening of the new school in 1857, the building became a reading room and then a cottage where Presbyterians held a service on every other Sunday afternoon. The Green now consists of two cottages: windows have replaced two redundant doors and two extra windows have been added. The large tree in front of the cottages has gone and the small horse-chestnut tree on the extreme left has developed into a magnificent specimen, which now hides the houses of The Mains, which can be seen on the left. Families still come from miles around for the famous Simonburn conkers.

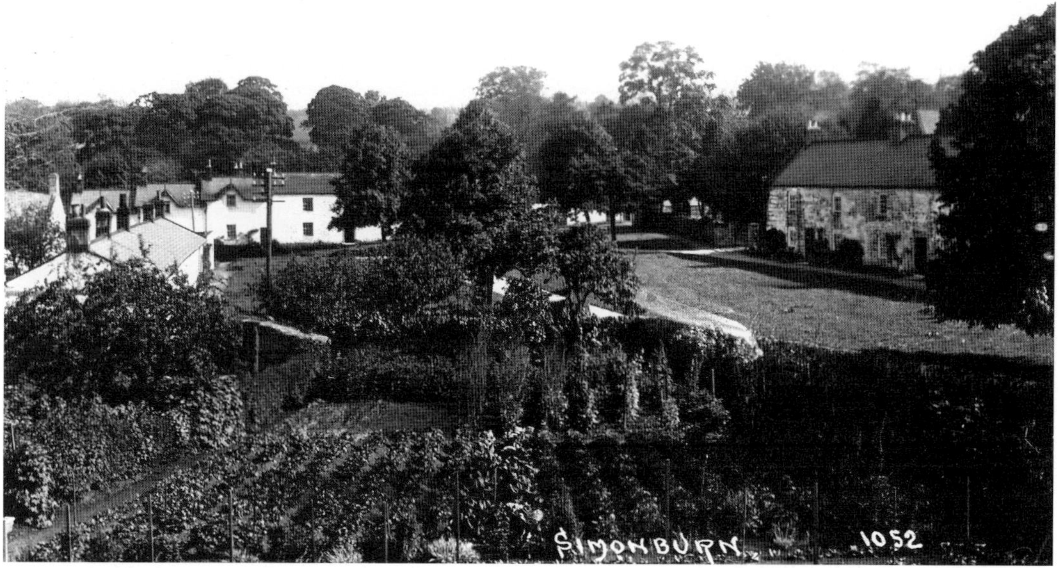


**SIMONBURN** This south-facing picture was taken in front of the shop & post office of Frank Watson Smith (1852-1930), postmaster for over 40 years. Facing each other across the village green are traditional cottages, now painted in Nunwick grey, a reminder that most of Simonburn is an estate village. The Green is on the left and on the right is Rectory Terrace. Directly ahead is Red Lion Terrace, at the end of which, nearest the church, was the Red Lion Inn, once famous for brewing its own ale, where a list of the Simonburn Floral and Horticultural Society hung. The inn closed around 1875, a likely victim of the Temperance Movement, which was popular among estate owners of the 19th century. Simonburn post office, shop and tearoom still stand at the western end of The Mains, a line of four Victorian houses, each with its own garden.

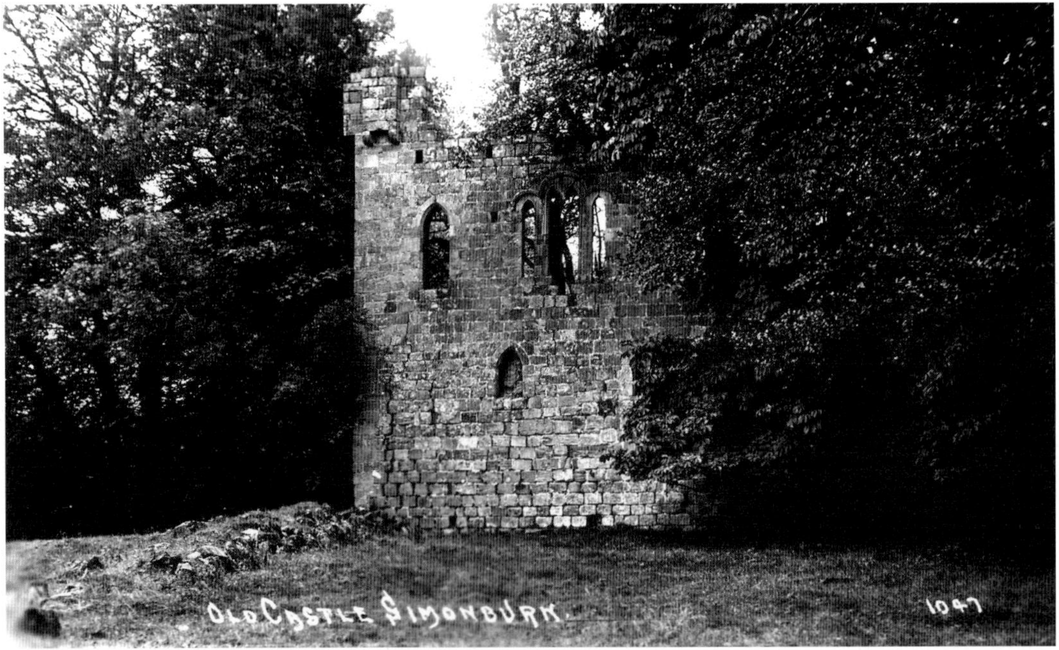


**SIMONBURN** The castle is first mentioned in 1415 but traces of an earlier motte and bailey are recorded. This single tower was built on elevated ground between the Castle Burn to the north and the road to Fenwickfield to the south but had been abandoned by the Heron family from the mid-16th century. John Wallis records that, in the earlier part of the 18th century, the legend that treasure was buried in the castle led to its demolition *to satisfy a violent curiosity* of the country people. In 1766, Sir Lancelot Allgood rebuilt the upper part of the east wall of the castle and two angular turrets as an eyecatcher for the Nunwick Estate. The east wall is now derelict and displays the damage that 80 years have wrought since this picture was taken. The window stones have been removed and placed on the ground some distance from the castle.

**BELLINGHAM** had been the home of W. P. Collier (1875-1937) for about four years before the outbreak of the Great War, in which he himself served between 1917 and 1919 as a photographer with the Royal Flying Corps. In March 1919, he was elected secretary of the Bellingham post of the Comrades of the Great War and his name appears amongst those who served on the lych gate of Bellingham cemetery. W. P. Collier rarely spoke about his wartime service but did confess to dropping the occasional glass plate because his fingers were numbed by cold. He was, however, in Bellingham to record the key events that marked the beginning and end of the conflict. Britain declared war on Germany at 12.15 a.m. on 5th August 1914. A few hours later, he was recording the muster of the B (Bellingham) Company of the 4th Battalion Northumberland Fusiliers, under the command of Captain E. C. Dixon and Lieutenant Goodall, outside the Bellingham armoury in Fountain Terrace and their departure by train. The Hexham Courant of 8th August 1914 recorded that *the local members of the 4th Battalion Northumberland Fusiliers, called out on mobilisation, were mustered and marched to the station, there to entrain for Hexham to join the other units of the Battalion that were gathering at the headquarters previous to their departure for the east. The men had an enthusiastic send off, though there were some affecting scenes.* Poignantly also, he recorded the muster of horses from local farms for military transport purposes. The Hexham Courant of 24th October 1914 noted that the requirements of the Army authorities had denuded the district of many of its horses and in some directions the scarcity was being felt, as there were *no horses for the ambulance to take patients to the hospital without, in some instances, considerable delay.* Amid great rejoicing, however, he recorded the Peace Celebrations of Saturday 19th July 1919, the day chosen for the national celebration of victory and peace. Even the inmates of the Bellingham Workhouse were entertained to high tea. The Children's Peace Tea was postponed until Thursday 4th September because the Peace Mugs did not arrive on time. The funeral of W. P. Collier on 11th September 1937 was attended by a large contingent of the local British Legion with their standard, together with a large number of family and friends and representatives of the Burns Club. His coffin was covered by a Union Jack and the Last Post and Reveille were sounded at the graveside. The standard of the British Legion was lowered while poppies were dropped into the grave.

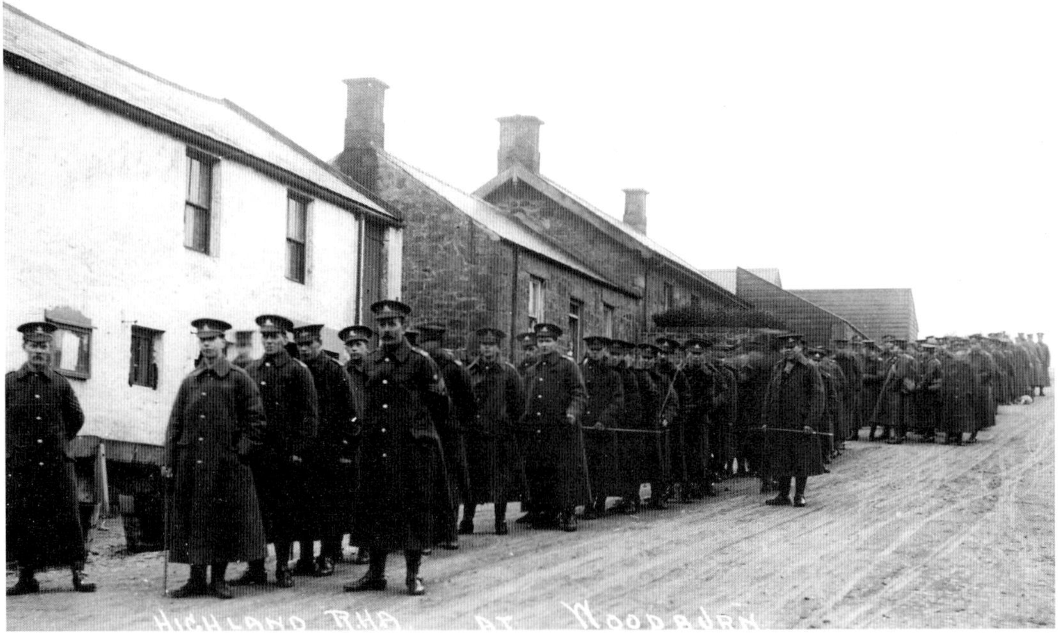


**HIGHLAND RHA** The First World War saw great activity at railway stations like Woodburn and Bellingham, where troops with their horses and equipment were regularly disembarked for military training. Having marched down the steep bank at West Woodburn from the station, a contingent of the Royal Horse Artillery pauses outside the Fox & Hounds Hotel before continuing its 10-mile march to Rochester and the Redesdale Artillery Range, which opened in March 1911. The hotel was a smallholding and included the smithy and two cottages with the adjacent fields. The Fox & Hounds closed in January 2000 and is now called Brandy Bank House, offering refreshments and accommodation. Brandy Bank is said to have got its name when a barrel of brandy rolled off a cart as it was being smuggled across the Border.

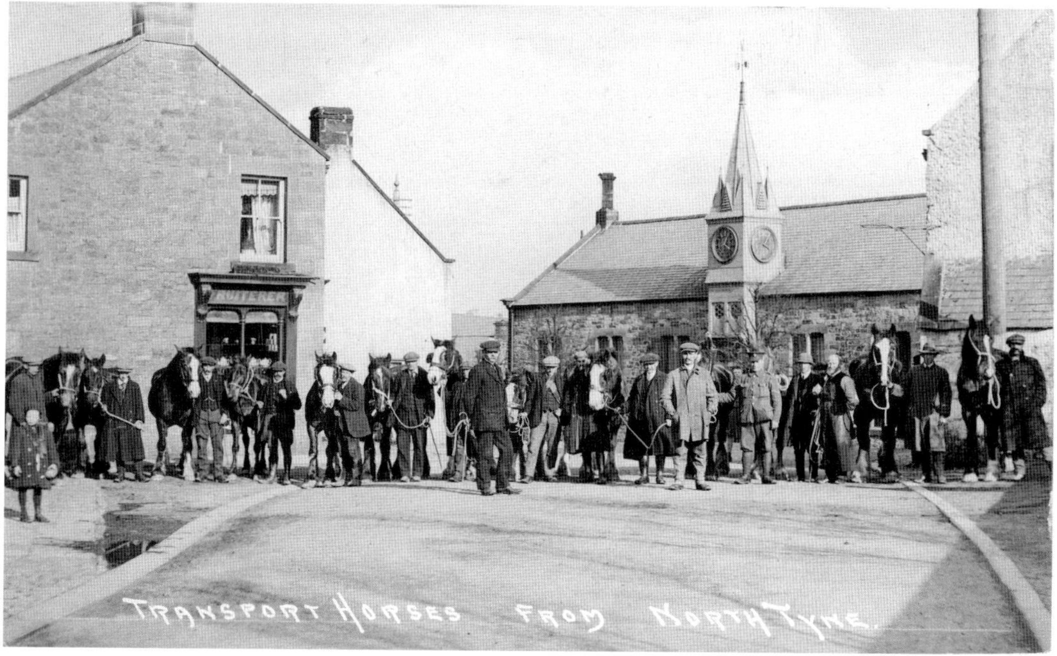


**TRANSPORT HORSES** On 5th August 1914, Captain Robinson and Lieutenant Bell of the Territorial Army established the Abbey Grounds in Hexham for the first wave of the purchase and inspection of transport horses. The net was soon cast wider and this picture, taken in the autumn of 1914 near Bellingham Town Hall, shows the farmers of the North Tyne with the horses that the Army had requisitioned. Two horses right of the shop window stands, halter in hand, Thomas Thompson of Greenhaugh, a cartman, who farmed a small piece of land. He had several horses but losing even one would have been a great sacrifice. It was all the more poignant because, despite assurances to the contrary, people knew that their horses, which were their means of earning a living and their faithful friends, would never be coming back.

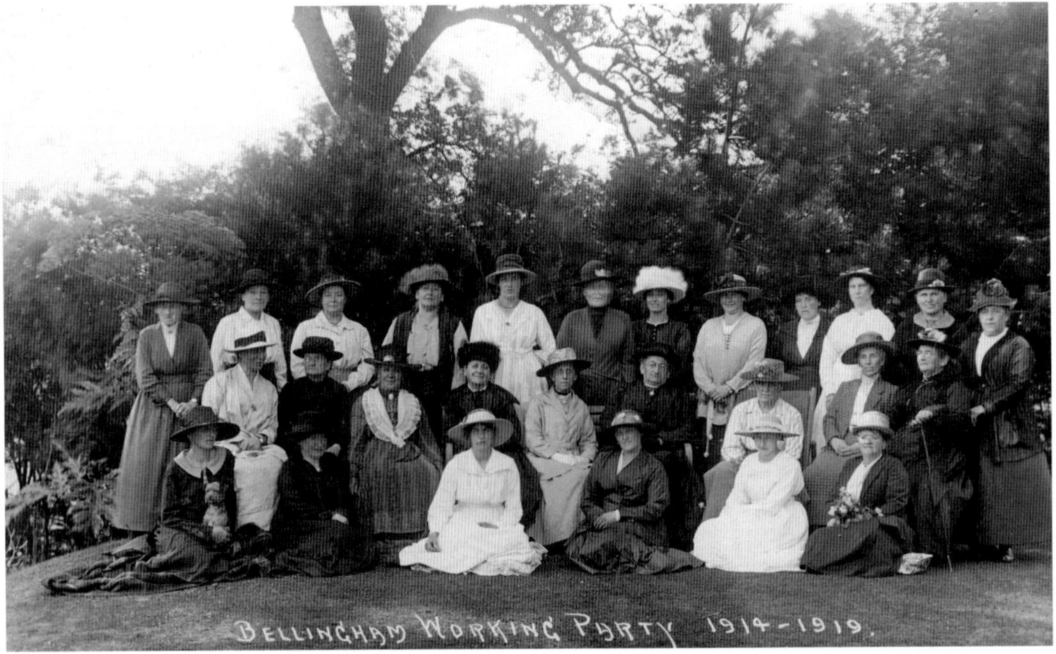


**WORKING PARTY** On 15th March 1919, W. P. Collier was elected secretary of the new Bellingham post of the Comrades of the Great War and was duly asked to forward to the Bellingham Ladies' Working Party a letter of thanks, published in the Hexham Courant of 3rd May 1919: … *nothing was left undone to ensure our comfort and well-being. We were regaled with tobacco, cigarettes, chocolates, sweets, cakes and Oxo, and at Christmas time we had your delicious home made plum puddings. Over and above these, you distributed more than 10,000 articles of underwear, gloves, etc, etc. Such effort must have called for great self-sacrifice, both in time, money and material, and we want you to know that your endeavours on our behalf touched our hearts and many times helped us to stiffen a lip and stifle a grouse …*

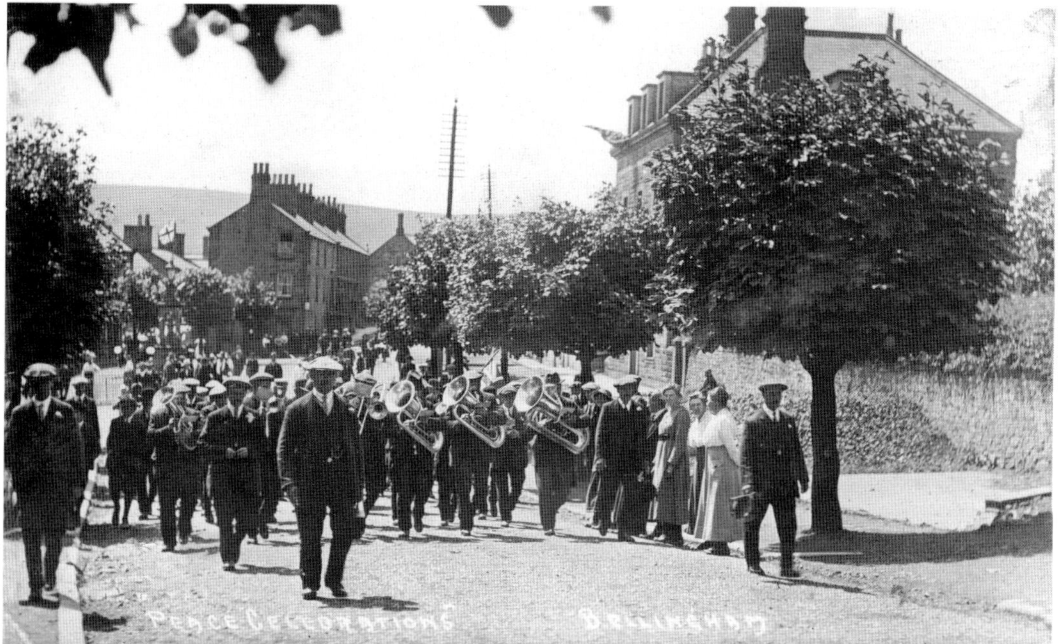


**PEACE CELEBRATIONS** W. P. Collier served in the Great War as an aerial photographer from July 1917 to March 1919 and his record of 19th July 1919, the day of national rejoicing, captures the relief that followed the Armistice. The Heworth Colliery Prize Silver Band headed a grand procession to the Fairstead, where a programme of sports and games was held and free teas were given to more than 1,000 local people, including the inmates of the Bellingham Workhouse. A dance followed until 8.30 p.m. when the singing of Auld Lang Syne and the National Anthem ended the first part of the celebrations. At 11 p.m. a large crowd saw two of the oldest men in the parish, James Aynsley (84) and Joseph Breckons (83), light a bonfire, which was topped by an effigy of the Kaiser. The celebrations ended with the National Anthem.

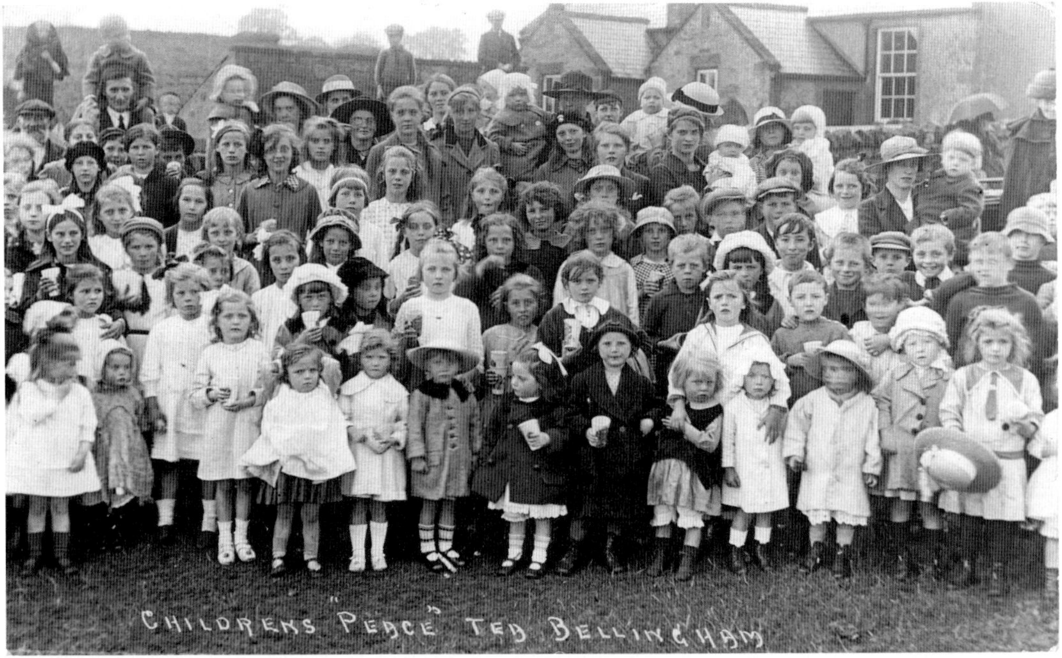


**PEACE TEA** This was held on 4th September 1919, some time after the official celebrations of 19th July, because of a delay in obtaining the peace mugs, which some of the children are proudly holding in their hands. Children under 14 years of age assembled near the golf course, where the ladies of the committee provided an excellent tea, with sweets and chocolates being provided by Mrs. T. Johnson of Percy Street. After tea came a sports competition and money prizes were awarded. The children gave three cheers for the ladies of the Peace Celebration Committee, who included Mrs. F. Potts, Mrs. C. Maughan, Mrs. Breckons, Mrs. E. W. Robson, Mrs. Simmonds, Mrs. R. Hedley, Miss Pigg, Miss N. Potts and Miss L. Armstrong, Reedsmouth. The arrangements were carried out by Mr. R. Hedley, secretary, and Mr. A. Smith, treasurer.

**ELSDON** stands before its 14th century Pele Tower and church of St. Cuthbert. Modern developments have done little to disturb the old-fashioned atmosphere of this ancient village and its seven-acre village green, one of the largest in England. When the Duchess of Northumberland opened the Elsdon fete, held in aid of the Church Restoration Fund, on 11th September 1926, she observed that Elsdon was one of the prettiest and most romantic villages in all Northumberland. Cottages with brilliant gardens stood round three sides of a square and a wonderful steep of healthy pasturage rose up from the fourth. Gleaming white geese gobbled on the greenest of grass commons and the centuries-old church had been like a golden thread appearing again and again in the fabric of the romantic history of Northumberland. The Duke and Duchess walked to the church, where they were amused by the collection of bushes that grew precariously in the crevices of the belfry. Inside, where the windows were beautiful and the walls a rich, wonderful brown, they read through the long list of Rectors of Elsdon, which began with William Brito in 1200 A.D. The medieval village became a centre for drovers in the 18th and 19th centuries, where *faws* or *tinklers* frequently rendezvoused on the moor near Elsdon and amidst the neighbouring wilds eluded the restraints of law and committed their depredations with impunity. Three inns, the Crown, Bacchus and Bird in Bush could slake the most persistent thirsts but their fortunes waned as the drovers left and Elsdon was bypassed by the Ponteland turnpike from Belsay to Otterburn, which was completed in 1836. Bulmer, in his History and Directory of Northumberland (1886), briefly observed that *the village now consists of the church, rectory house, a temperance hotel, a grocer's shop, and a few cottages. Formerly it had its weekly market on Tuesday and an annual fair on the 26th August, but both of these have long been obsolete, though the privileges of the last are still maintained by the yearly custom of riding the boundaries and proclaiming the fair in dumb show.* An 18th century pinfold for stray cattle and sheep still stands on the large village green and, until 1974, children would run around the perimeter as the Marathon on their School Sports Day. In the 1960s, the village was popular with day-trippers and the old Bacchus Inn reopened as a teashop. Only the Bird in Bush Inn now survives and a teashop in the old school house. The atmosphere of this historic village is unique and still has the power to charm the most casual visitor.

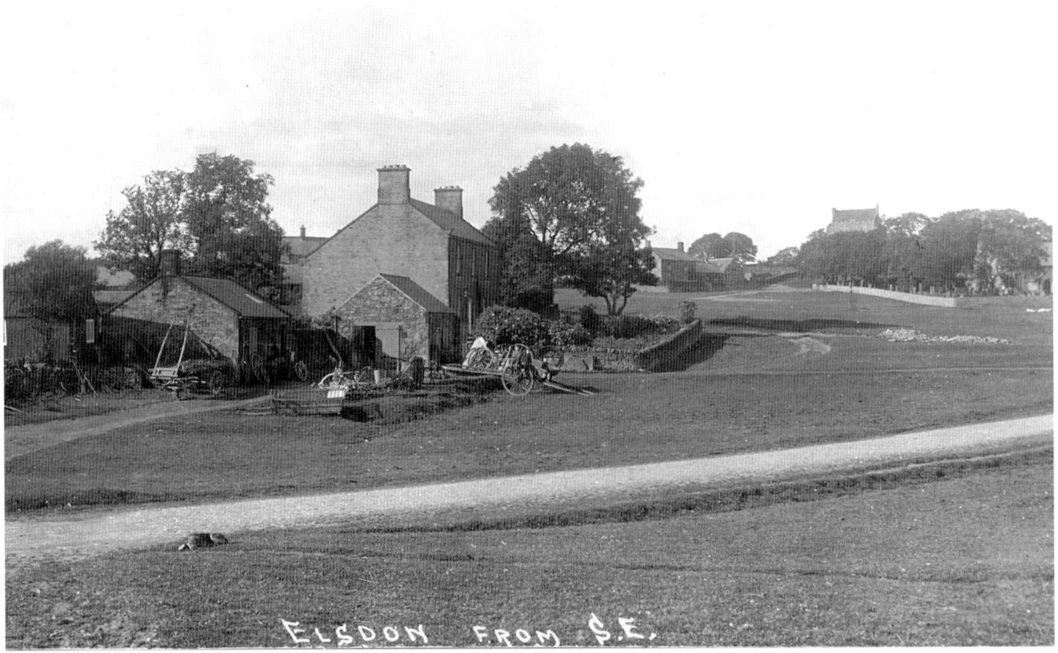


**ELSDON** Carts and wheels lie strewn outside the smithy of John Ormiston (1889-1960), who succeeded his father George Ormiston (1848-1910) as blacksmith. When he moved to new premises behind the Percy Arms at Otterburn around 1925, the smithy became the cobbler's shop of Archibald Rutherford Potts (1872-1955), brother of Donald Robert Potts (1870-1945), who lived at Blue House Cottage. For 18 years, the nearer house on the left was White Hall Post Office, which Eliza Mary Hedley, the eldest daughter of George and Jane Hedley, ran until her father, who lived next door, died aged 92 on 27th May 1926. White Hall had once been a single property with a Presbyterian meeting-room upstairs. Isabella Storey (1885-1958) continued as postmistress but, after several moves around Elsdon, the post office closed in April 1999.

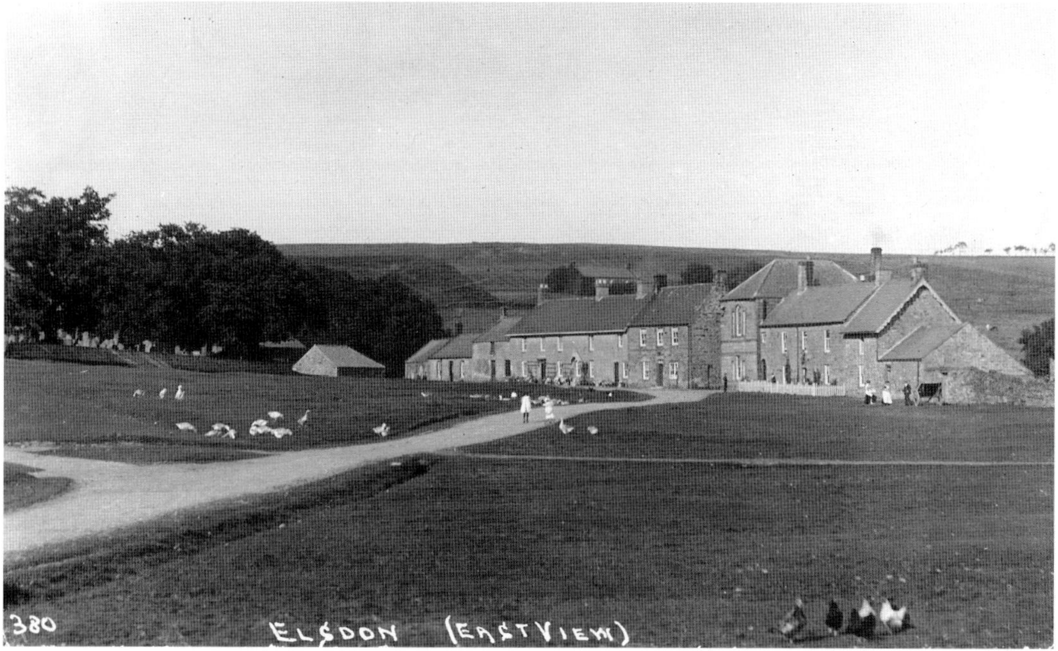


**ELSDON** The village had three inns in the 19th century but only the Bird in Bush survives. On the left is the Crown Inn, with the inscription John Gallon 1729, which later became a Temperance Inn and was run for several generations by the Keith family. An upper storey was added to the old coach house next to the Crown, where Allan (1873-1940) and Susanna (1881-1949) Easton, brother and sister, had their grocery shop. The first floor of the tall building next door was a Presbyterian meeting-room. Behind the white fencing is the Bacchus Inn, dating from 1730, which closed in the mid-19th century but still has a statue of the Greek god of wine over the door. The building on the far left was a hay barn, which Michael Storey demolished for the site of his house, Braeside, which he built in 1925 for himself and his wife Elizabeth.

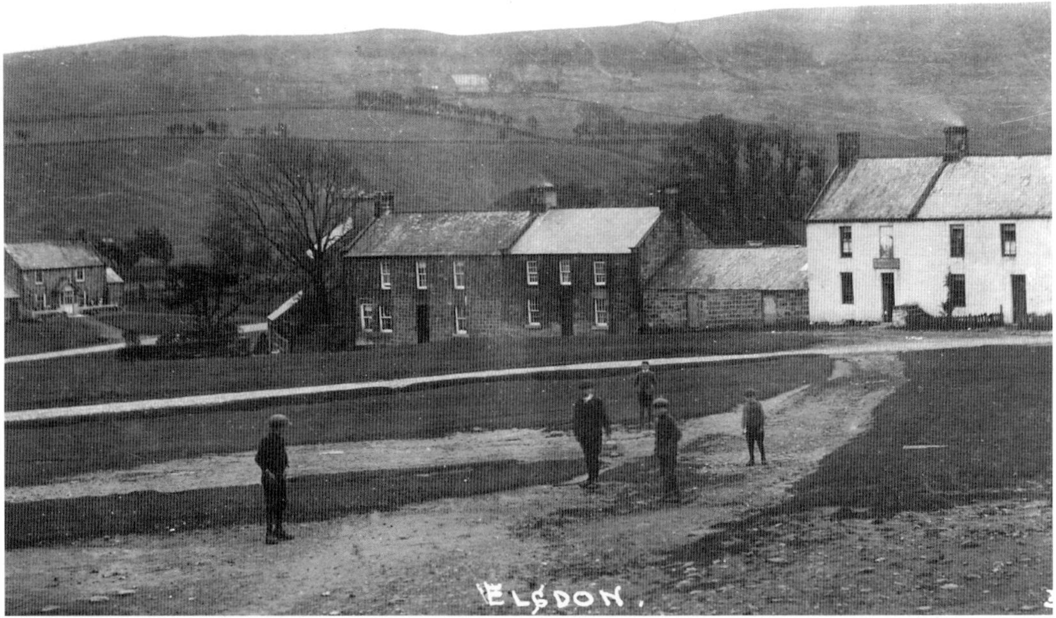


**ELSDON** Children stand on the path leading to the Bird in Bush and look towards the camera of W. P. Collier. For almost forty years, John Whaley (1817-1890) was the proprietor of this hostelry and his daughter, Mary Ann Whaley (1860-1909), ran the inn after the death of her father. Bernard Brannan (1864-1932) and his wife Barbara (1866-1951) succeeded her and for more than thirty years the Bird in Bush carried the name of Brannan over the door, with Barbara continuing to run the inn for ten years after the death of her husband on 19th August 1932. Sam Ramshaw converted the single-storey byre on the left in the late 1980s into the poolroom and toilets. In the late 1990s, Lesley Marshall, seeking to extend the facilities of this village local, converted the former snug and kitchen on the right into what is now a pleasant dining room.

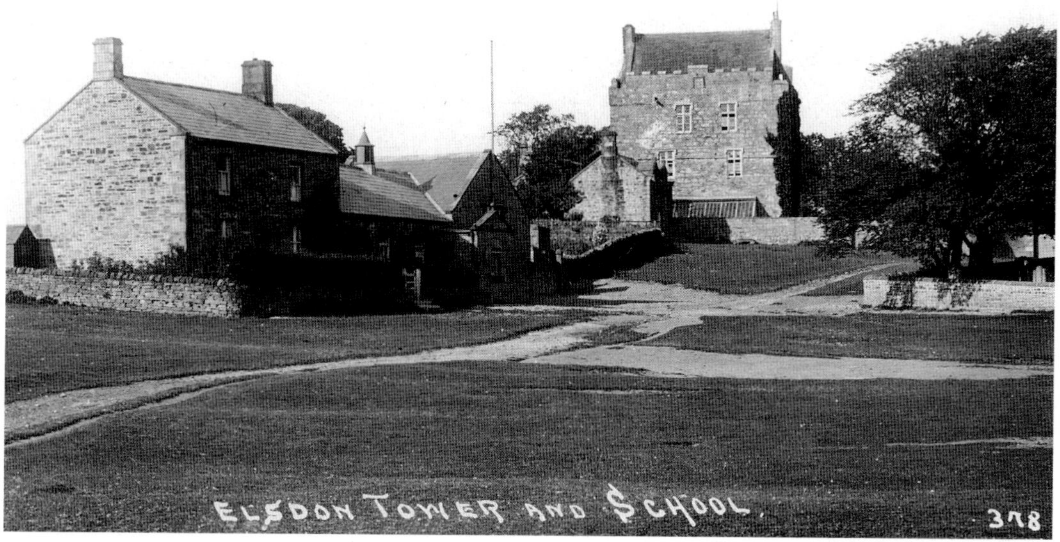


**ELSDON** On the left of this view is Elsdon school house, originally a single-storey thatched farmhouse called Tod House farm, and next door stands Elsdon School, opened in 1835 as the Rector's School. The school had around 55 pupils in the 1930s but evacuees from Tyneside swelled numbers in the Second World War and a classroom was opened at the top of Elsdon Tower. Electric light arrived on 19th January 1939 and school dinners were first served on 1st May 1947. Numbers fell after the War and the school closed in 1974 with 29 pupils on the roll, the last entry in the School Log describing Sports Day on 12th July. September saw Elsdon pupils transferred to the County First School at Otterburn. For several years, the old school was the Newcastle Diocesan Youth Centre and dormitories were built on the north side.

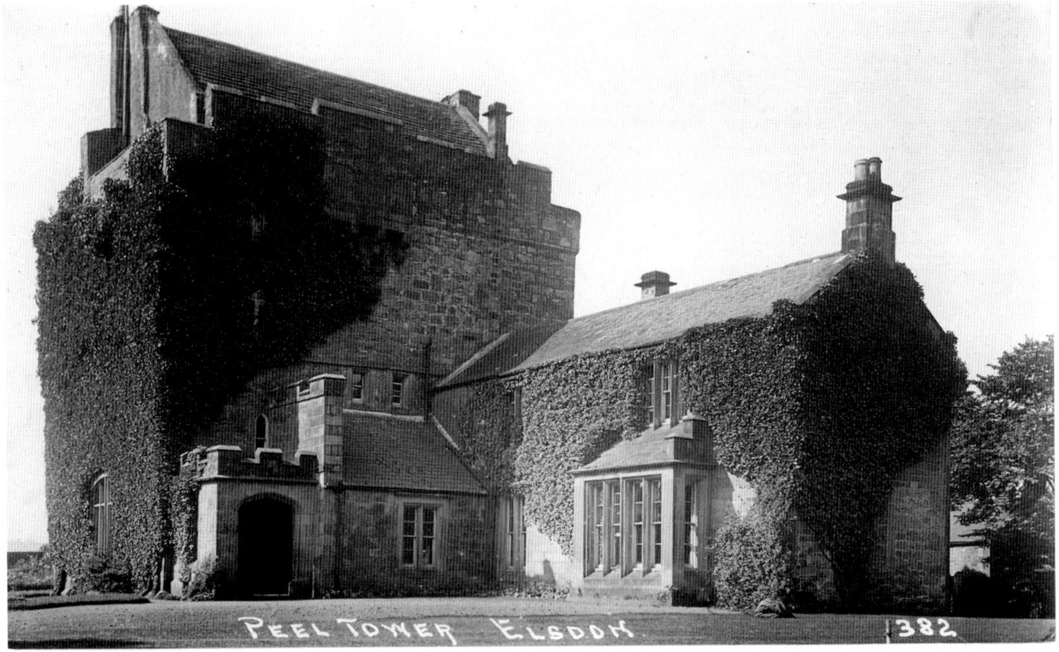


**ELSDON** This striking Pele Tower dates from the 14th century and was probably built by the Umfraville family at the same time as the church to protect the villagers from marauding bands. Animals were sheltered on the ground floor, which has walls eight feet thick, and people took refuge above. From 1415, the local rector was housed in the tower. The Reverend Thomas Singleton added the attached house after 1812. It continued as a rectory until 1961 and then became the home of church organist Mary (1911-1984) and George Taylor (1909-1991), who wrote a history of Elsdon. The original road probably went past the tower to cross the Elsdon Burn by the old sandstone bridge to continue past Elsdon Mill to Rothbury. Elsdon Tower has been stripped of its creeper to reveal the restored stonework of this private residence.

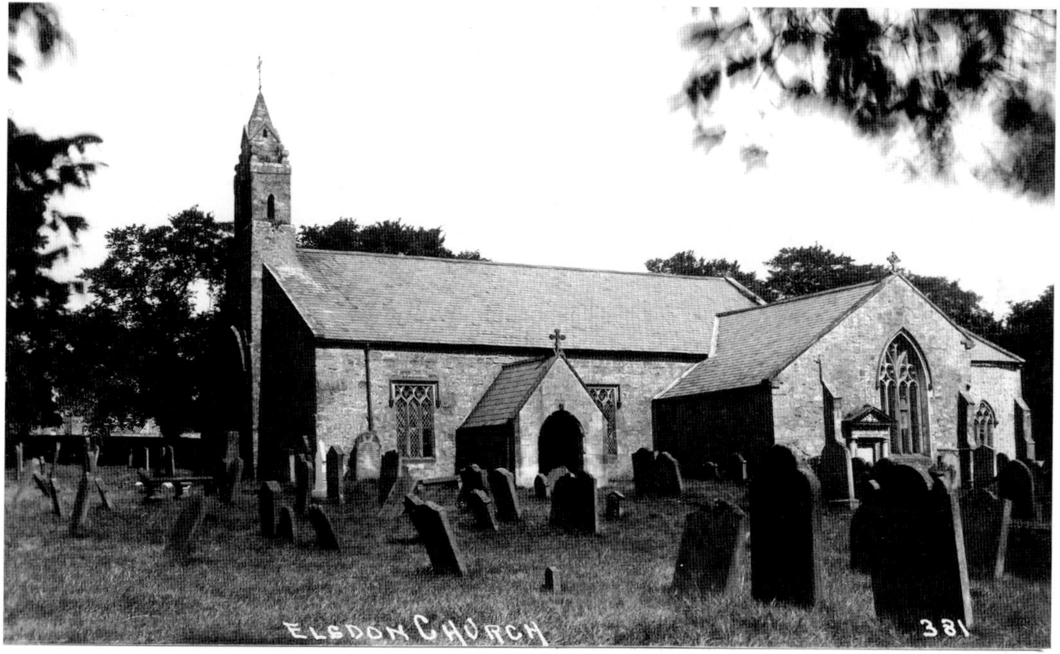


**ELSDON** St. Cuthbert's Church is the mother church of Redesdale and dates from the 14th century, though there are traces of an earlier 11th or 12th century building. The bones of St. Cuthbert are said to have rested here in 875 on their long journey from Lindisfarne. Displayed within the church is a tombstone describing in unique detail the career of a Roman tribune, who died, aged 48 years, 6 months and 25 days, while serving at the Roman fort of Bremenium at High Rochester. His wife, Julia Lucilla, dedicated this memorial to her husband, whose name was probably Rufinus. On display also are the skulls of three horses, discovered inside the spire that surmounts the bell turret, during the 1877 restoration. Their purpose is uncertain. Most of the church windows are plain glass and the graveyard contains headstones of great antiquity.

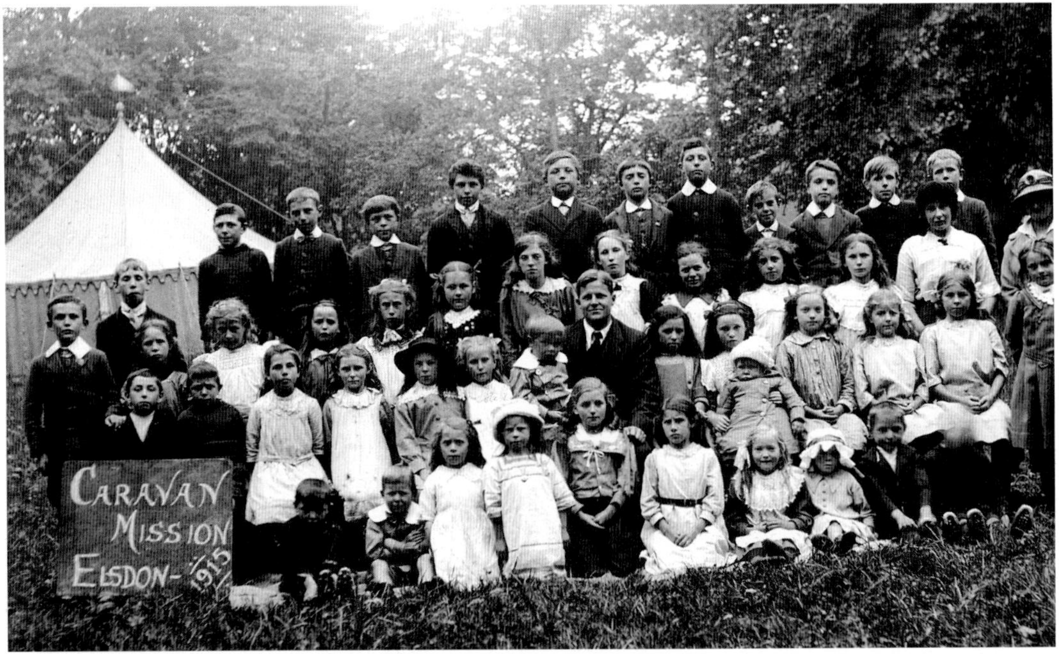


**CARAVAN MISSION** Hugh James, a London missioner, sits with children from the area around Elsdon in August 1915. The Caravan Mission to Village Children developed from the Children's Special Service Mission, founded in 1867 by Joseph Spiers. The first Caravan Mission took place in 1893, using a baker's cart to reach areas where churches or people were so scattered that the Gospel was not reaching them. The Mission was most active during the summer, when the weather was fine and the children were on holiday. Missioners would stay in one village for a week or two before moving to another. They were given a horse-drawn square caravan with a couple of bunks, a small tent for cooking and a marquee, which they would erect in a convenient field, where children and parents could hear the Gospel and sing hymns.

**PEGGY DENT** has lived her whole life in Elsdon. She was born on 25th May 1920 at the Whitlees, the shepherd's cottage for Whiskershiel, the farm of her grandparents, Thomas and Elizabeth Carruthers. She was the fourth child of Mary (née Nichol) and Thomas Usher Carruthers, who had five daughters and one son. Her father was born at Townhead near Hawick and her mother was born in Upper Coquetdale at Dykeham's Edge, a farm that was abandoned in 1938 and used as a target on the Redesdale Artillery Range. After both of her grandparents died in 1931, the family left the Whitlees and moved into Whiskershiel. Peggy married Albert Dent in 1940 and moved back to the Whitlees. When he was called up, shortly after the birth of their son Arthur, she left the Whitlees and spent the rest of the War at Whiskershiel. After the War, their daughter Maureen was born and they took one of the Elsdon Council Houses, built in 1938, and Albert worked at Elsdon pit. In 1961, they moved back into Whiskershiel to look after Peggy's parents. They left shortly after her father died in 1971 and bought the Pinfold Cottage Shop. They gave the shop up in 1985 but continued to live in Pinfold Cottage.

"My father was a good musician and played the fiddle. Both mother and father were keen readers of authors like Dickens and Burns and they would read any books that they had over and over again. Newspapers were sent by post and would be passed around and read from cover to cover. We would often squabble about who would get to read them first. My father used to sit in his chair and read but my mother had a book propped up on the table and would be knitting socks as she read, never looking at what she was doing. Sometimes she would knit the foot of a sock far too long and would have to pull it out because she was so intent on her reading.

I was about eight when my grandfather got the wireless, a huge box with a great horn on the top. A wire went through the side of the window to a large aerial on the roof. One day, the aerial got struck by lightening and it came right down into the house. My little brother Thomas, who was about four at the time, was sitting on a chest by the wireless and the lightening came down the wire through the window and shot across the floor past his toes. He was wearing a pair of rubber-soled sandals and the toes of the sandals were burnt. Two working lads, who were sitting at the table having a meal, were jerked up and their knees caught the bottom of the table. The lightening did not do the wireless much good either!

My grandparents kept a horse and trap and every Sunday my grandmother, who was quite religious, would get dressed up and ride to Otterburn Presbyterian Church, weather permitting. Sunday was a day of rest. Nothing was done, unless it was absolutely necessary, and nothing was read, except the Bible or a magazine called Sunday at Home. My parents were not so strict. Christmas was more or less ignored. I cannot remember Christmas cards or presents. We had dolls and toys, of course, but they were all wooden and made at home.

My grandfather later had a car and we would sometimes drive to the shops in Rothbury but we did not need to go shopping very much because travellers would come to the farm. Howard Graham, son of Matthew Graham, came from his shop in Ridsdale to deliver our monthly grocery order. Francis Brinton came on horseback every so often from Blayney's of Newcastle, from where we used to get a chest full of tea. We got flour for making bread and cakes from another carrier who came round monthly. Jimmy Oliver, a draper, used to come over from Hexham and usually stayed overnight. Another draper, Jack Mowitt, came from Rothbury. Another traveller rode from Hawick on his bicycle and sold lengths of tweed, which he wrapped up in oilskin and strapped to the carrier on the back. He could only carry four or five rolls because they were so big. You chose the cloth that you wanted and he would get it made up into a suit. Vans would come into Elsdon every day, grocers, fruiterers, butchers, bakers and general travellers.

One of my earliest memories, when we were at the Whitlees, is of the local carrier. He came once a week with his pony and a flat cart and always had a little treat for us children. I think that he was called Mr. Wright and he exchanged any spare butter and eggs for fruit or a few groceries. We grew our own potatoes and vegetables and produced our own bacon and eggs, which we always had with fried bread for breakfast. Our postman was called Jack Jennings but he did not come up every day. He would wait until he had things worth delivering.

We made our own fun at home. We were a big family and always seemed to have lots of people around, especially for musical evenings. Other families would have cardings at Christmas when people played cards for geese and turkeys. We worked hard and played hard. We had a good life and never thought much about money. Neighbours helped neighbours. You could rely on them. You never thought, "Oh, I'll get such and such for doing this."

My mother could turn her hand to almost anything but she had a full time job in the house, cleaning, washing and cooking. She cooked on an open range with a big oven, heated by coal. The coal came from Elsdon pit and everyone would help to lead it back on the horse and cart. People used to come from miles around to collect their coal from the pit, with three or four horses and carts together. I can just remember the men cutting peat near the Whitlees but the quality was poor and we did not use it much.

I walked three miles to Elsdon School. It had about 75 pupils. I remember Jean Milburn and three headmasters, Daniel Harrison, John Short and Thomas Harvey. We started with scripture in the morning and games. The Rector held a service on Friday morning. We had arithmetic and mental arithmetic, history and geography, reading and poetry, music and singing, English and spelling tests, science and nature study, when we went on nature walks, and a school garden. I liked school, especially the gardening and nature walks. My favourite subjects were arithmetic, reading and spelling but not sewing because my needle was always sticking in the cloth.

The teachers were very strict. One teacher had a cane and knew how to use it. Another had a cat o' nine tails, a strap, and used it on our arms or the back of our legs. I sometimes got punished for talking or getting up to mischief but never for my lessons. We had to go to church on special days like Ascension Day or Good Friday. If there was a funeral, we were not allowed to play beside the church. We had to stay in school and keep quiet. In the holidays, all the children were expected to help out on the farm.

As soon as I left school, I worked at Whiskershiel. Monday was washing day. We had a big wash-house and in the corner was a set-pot, which had to be filled up with water the night before. Long bars of hard soap had to be sliced up and put into the boiler the night before so that they softened. Then we lit the fire under the boiler and waited until the water heated up. We had two barrels with poss-sticks. We lifted the hot water out of the set-pot into the barrels and then cleaned the clothes in the first barrel with the poss-sticks. We wrung them out by hand and then scrubbed them on the table. Then we put them into the second barrel, possed the clothes again, and then wrung them out. By that time, the first barrel was empty and so you filled it up with cold water, rinsed the clothes, wrung them out again and hung them on the line to dry.

Tuesday was ironing day. We had flat irons that we heated up in the fire and box irons. Wednesday was the day when we cleaned the bedrooms. Thursday was baking day and we used to bake about a dozen loaves, scones, cakes and teacakes. Friday was the day for scrubbing out the dairy and pantry and black-leading the huge iron range in the kitchen. Saturday was for scrubbing all the floors. On Sunday, when we got older, we went to church once a month in the Long Room next door to the Bacchus in Elsdon. We stayed with my great aunts near Hawick for our summer holidays. Every night, they would read a passage from the Bible and we had to sit as quiet as mice listening.

Four weeks of non-stop work began with the lambing in April. The men were kept busy because the sheep were spread all over the 1,200 acres of Whiskershiel. If the sheep needed attention after they had their lambs, they would go and bring them in. We would feed the weak lambs with bottles. There were no tractors. It was all about driving the sheep and having patience. The clipping started in the summer. The sheep would be clipped by hand with shears. We rolled up the fleeces ready for the wool sacks but left filling them until it was a wet day. In later years, all the farms would get together for the clipping, which was hard work but great fun.

After the clipping came haymaking time. Whoever was cutting the hay would get up at about 4 o'clock in the morning and get the horse yoked into the reaper and get the hay cut before it got too hot for the horse. Then it was all hand raking and hand forking. Then we put the hay into the hay shed. If we had a good crop and there was too much to go into the hay shed, we made haystacks, but we filled the hay shed first. After haymaking, it was a matter of sorting out the sheep to go to the marts. Life on the farm ticked over during the year, with the routine jobs that had to be done. When winter came on, the cattle were brought inside and needed feeding. We usually had eight or ten milking cows and half a dozen calves. We sent most of our sheep to Rothbury. I can remember, when I was very small, that my father used to drive the sheep over the fell to Rothbury. He never used the road. The auctioneer had fields where people could keep their sheep the night before the mart. My father used to stay overnight and then walk back from the mart on the next day. The shepherds from the Coquet did the same but, by the time of the Second World War, we would take our stock to the mart by lorry.

My grandfather kept a hemmel just for the tramps who came by Whiskershiel. He always put clean hay inside as bedding. Whole families would come and stay overnight and he always made sure that they got fed. One old lady, in particular, was treated as a bit special because she was allowed to come up to the farmhouse and stay in a calf pen, if there was one empty. We would give her some clean bedding or a blanket and she would stay for a few days. She would always do crochet work and give a bit of crochet lace, or something, to my mother. She came for years and must have been quite well off at one time. Another man, who used to come regularly, always had a book in his pocket. He must have been a bit of a scholar because he always carried his book and was very polite. We did not expect the tramps to do any jobs in return for their stay with us. They got food and shelter and then moved on the next day. They would come up to the farmhouse and ask if they could have a kettle boiled and we usually gave them a sandwich. The tramps were supposed to put special marks along the road or on the trees so that the other tramps would know the places where they could stay. I suppose that Whiskershiel was so popular with the tramps because it had its own shelter.

The two grocery shops in Elsdon sold a little bit of everything, including paraffin, so you had to be careful not to get the groceries and the paraffin mixed. Allan Easton was in the old Coach House, next to the Crown, overlooking the village green. Susanna Easton, his sister, used to weigh out the sugar into blue sugar bags and sold tea, tobacco and cigarettes. One of my earliest memories, when I was at school, was when I would go to the shop to get tobacco for my grandfather and sometimes cigarettes for a lad who worked on the farm. A packet of 20 Players cigarettes cost 11½d. If I was lucky, I was given the halfpenny change out of the shilling. Jasper Familton had a shop in a hut at Low Mote. He was a carrier and had a garage and a charabanc, an open-topped bus with rails. I can still picture him driving round to take people to a wedding. His wife ran the shop and sold quite a lot of sweets. I remember that they had a bench with boxes of sweets for the bairns. There were sherbet dips, liquorice, little toffee bars, lollipops and gobstoppers. Some were a farthing and others cost a halfpenny. There was nothing over a penny. They also sold black bullets but they were more expensive. We always went to Mr. Familton for our sweets, as well as for tinned goods.

I married Albert Dent on 1st June 1940 in Elsdon Church. We held the reception at Whiskershiel with a dance in the village hall. We had our honeymoon in Keswick. After he was called up into the army, I left the Whitlees and went back to Whiskershiel to help my parents. One of the worst things about wartime was the blackout. We had to black out all of the windows and we were not allowed to carry lights. Rationing meant that everything was in short supply. We patched and darned clothing and made something from something else. Nothing was thrown away. We had to plough some of the land to grow feed for the stock. But the war did not stop us having fun. We had dances and functions to raise money for the troops or Red Cross. We cycled to the camp at Otterburn to see the latest pictures in the picture hall or hear the bands that came to entertain the troops. We always got in. Everyone was on the same side.

We left Whiskershiel shortly after my father died and bought the Pinfold Cottage Shop. It was a good business and I used to pride myself that I could supply almost anything, including advice, because people would come in to ask all sorts of questions. The newspapers were delivered about 6 o'clock in the morning and we opened about 8 o'clock. We had a lot of regular customers from the village and the local farms. People even came from Otterburn for their groceries. We used to get our stock once a week and travellers would come with all sorts of things. The baker came three times a week but he cut it down to twice a week, as fuel got more expensive. Sundays were very busy because we had the Sunday papers and people used to come regularly to Elsdon and picnic on the village green. The green used to be covered with people having picnics and children playing and having a grand time. But as the petrol went up in price, people stopped coming. I enjoyed the shop but I retired in 1985. Albert and I lived in Pinfold Cottage but we rented the shop to Harry Pearson, who added the post office.

Elsdon has changed a lot over the years. The post office and shops have all gone. The Rector left in 1961 and the pit closed in 1972. Elsdon School closed in July 1974. Harry Pearson gave up the shop and post office in April 1999. Elsdon used to have its own football club, youth club, Women's Institute and Mothers' Union. There was a reading room in the village hall. Over the years, all these have faded away. It is such a shame that almost everyone has to go out of the village to earn a living nowadays."

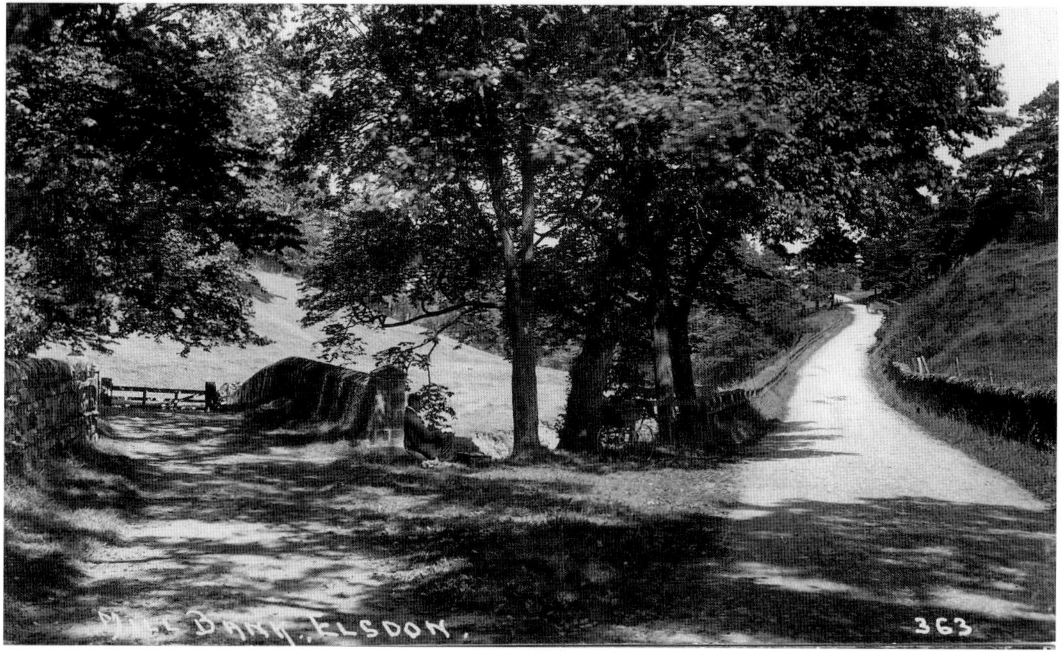


**ELSDON** Older Northumbrians can just recall the sight of W. P. Collier, wearing goggles and knickerbockers, with his camera and tripod strapped on his back and riding his 125cc Raleigh motorcycle along the country roads to take either bespoke family portraits or pictures to turn into postcards at his little shop in Bellingham. He liked nothing more than to leave the shop and take his pictures. Occasionally, the photographer or his motorcycle makes a cameo appearance and here W. P. Collier is pictured sitting against the old bridge over the Elsdon Burn, with the base of the Mote Hills on the right. These are the fine remains of an early 12th century motte and bailey castle, built of earth and timber, which Robert de Umfraville probably constructed, using local labour, to house his soldiers and impose his dominance over the local population.

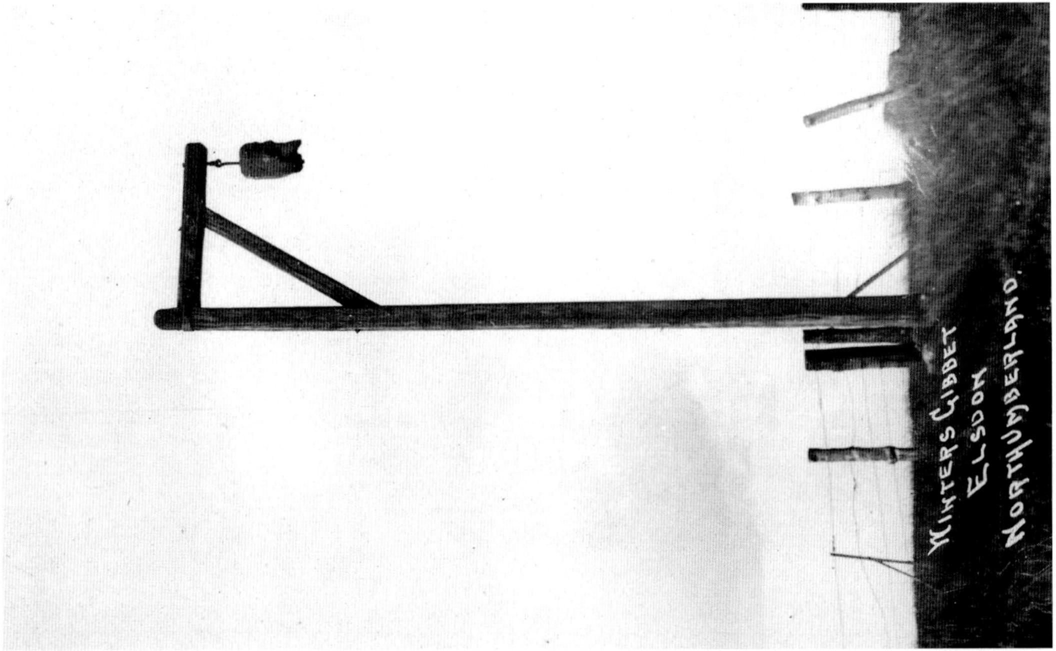


**ELSDON** On the evidence of a local shepherd boy, the body of William Winter was hung in chains within sight of The Raw farm, where on 29th August 1791 he and two accomplices had murdered and robbed Margaret Crozier, who kept a small shop for the sale of drapery and other goods. It was once believed that toothache could be cured by rubbing the bad tooth with chips of wood from the original gibbet. The latest replica head, unveiled on 6th April 1989, looks out over the most northerly part of the Wallington Estate from the same desolate spot on the summit of an old drove road. One mile further east, four trees, arranged in a rectangle on the south side of the road to Scots Gap, mark Shop Field, the site of a former smithy, where cattle were fitted with wooden shoes to enable them to be driven on metalled roads rather than grass tracks.

**WALLINGTON** and **CAMBO** are the jewels in the crown of the North Eastern region of the National Trust, whose offices are now in the former Temperance Hotel at Scots Gap, which until 13th September 1952 was a small railway junction that provided passengers with connections to Rothbury, Reedsmouth and Morpeth for the main LNER route to London. W. W. Tomlinson visited Cambo shortly after the improvements made by Sir Charles Edward Trevelyan (1809-1886) during his seven-year tenure of the Wallington Estate and in his Comprehensive Guide to Northumberland, published in 1888, he noted *several pretty dwelling houses and cottages, with gardens in front, the whole forming a picture of rustic peace and beauty not easily surpassed in the county.* Cambo was the subject of a research project conducted by the Cambo Women's Institute. In October 1921, a prize had been offered in the Women's Institute Journal for the best book compiled by a Women's Institute on local history. Members of the Cambo Women's Institute, which had been formed in 1919, entered this competition and, although they did not win first prize, they received a special award of two guineas. In 1929, their book, In the Troublesome Times, was edited and published. Edward Keith, who entered Wallington gardens as Indoor Assistant in 1882 and was Head Gardener between 1890 and 1933, read through the original manuscript before publication and made some additions. His long tenure of this important position at Wallington gave him unique authority. In his Memories of Wallington, privately printed in 1939, six years after his retirement, he gave a remarkable insight into the leading members of the Trevelyan family. The history of Cambo was continued in two subsequent publications of the Cambo Women's Institute in 1956 and in 1989, the 70th anniversary of their foundation, and their original book was also reprinted. A series of guides to Wallington followed its opening to the public by Sir Charles Philips Trevelyan (1870-1958) from Easter 1929, the most recent editions published by the National Trust. In 1984, Pauline Dower (1905-1988), who was the eldest of the six children of Sir Charles and Lady Trevelyan, published her Living at Wallington, in which she recalled her grandfather Sir George Otto Trevelyan and, after his death in 1928, the move from Cambo with her parents and her life at Wallington. On the death of her father, Sir Charles Philips Trevelyan, in 1958, the 13,000-acre Wallington Estate passed into the guardianship of the National Trust.

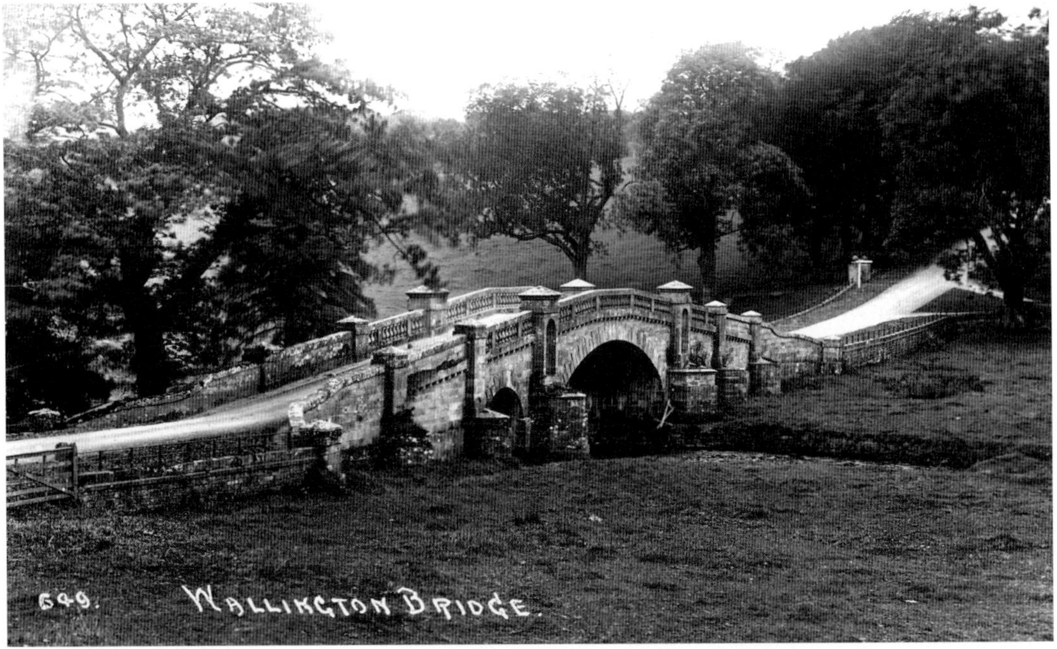


**WALLINGTON** The elegant hump-backed bridge that James Paine built across the River Wansbeck in 1755 is a memorial to Sir Walter Calverley Blackett (1707-1777), who inherited Wallington from his uncle Sir William Blackett in 1728. Sir Walter made Wallington his main residence and for almost fifty years had the wealth, vision, energy and enthusiasm to turn what had been a modest hunting lodge into one of the finest houses in Northumberland with an attached estate of 13,000 acres. He diverted the road to Cambo to the east of Wallington Hall as if to form a drive to the house. He employed the architect Daniel Garrett to turn Wallington into an elegant house and planted woods and gardens to provide a fine setting for both the house and the medieval village of Cambo, much of which he rebuilt as an estate village for his workers.

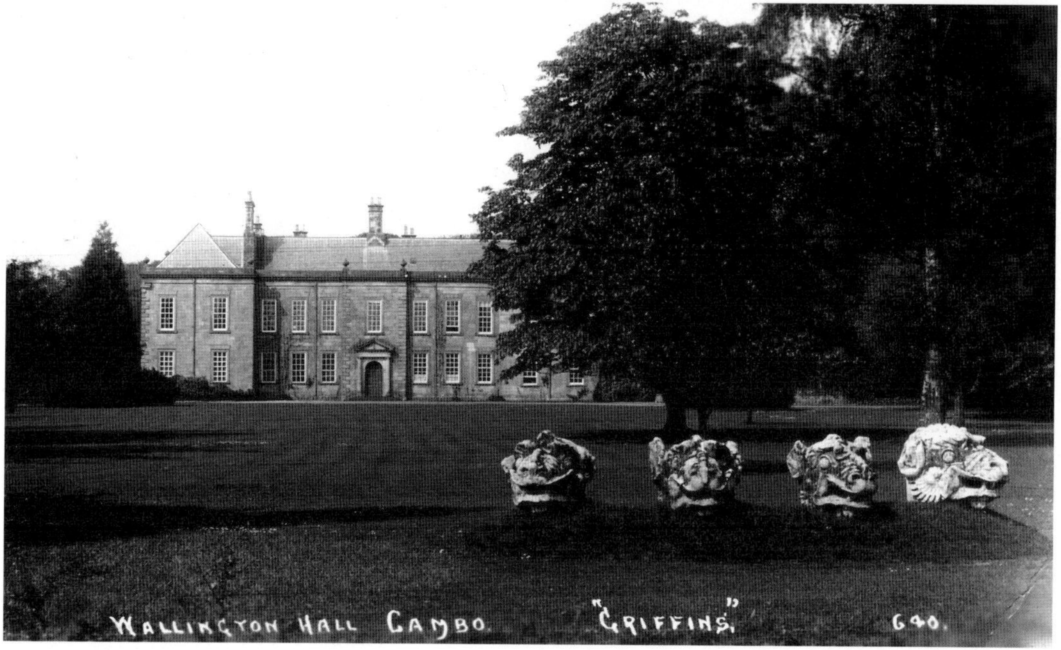


**WALLINGTON** Three leading families were associated with Wallington, the Fenwicks, Blacketts and Trevelyans, but the four grinning griffins on the east lawn of Wallington seem to celebrate the legacy of Sir Walter Calverley Blackett, M.P. for Newcastle, a wealthy merchant with interests in coal, lead mining and shipping, who began the development of the Wallington Estate that Sir Charles Philips Trevelyan conveyed to the National Trust in 1941 and which it has controlled since his death in 1958. In 1760, Sir Walter bought the griffins and some other sculptures from the demolition of Bishopsgate, one of the entrances to the City of London, to use as ballast in his ships. Sir Walter originally put the griffins on Rothley Crag, where he built a mock castle, but Sir Charles Philips Trevelyan placed them in their present position in 1928.

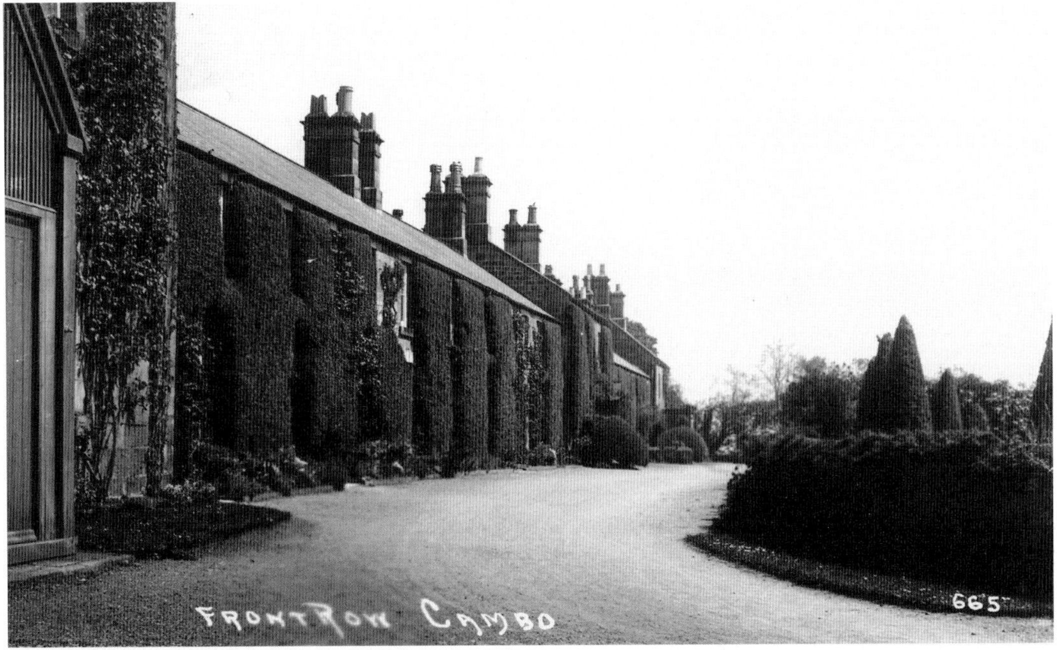


**CAMBO** This estate village consists of three Rows, Front, Middle and Back, now called North Row. Sir Walter Calverley Blackett built the eight single-storey cottages of Front Row, to which Sir Walter Calverley Trevelyan (1797-1879) added a second storey. They are framed by two of the five properties still owned by the Trevelyan family, Cambo House, furthest from the camera, and the Two Queens on the left, its wooden porch rebuilt in stone in 1952. Dating from 1760, the Two Queens was a coaching inn, so-called because its sign had Mary Queen of Scots facing north and Elizabeth I facing south. The inn was on a stagecoach route and had a large range of stables and outbuildings. Its days were numbered when Sir Walter Calverley Trevelyan, an ardent supporter of the Temperance Movement, inherited the Wallington Estate in 1846.

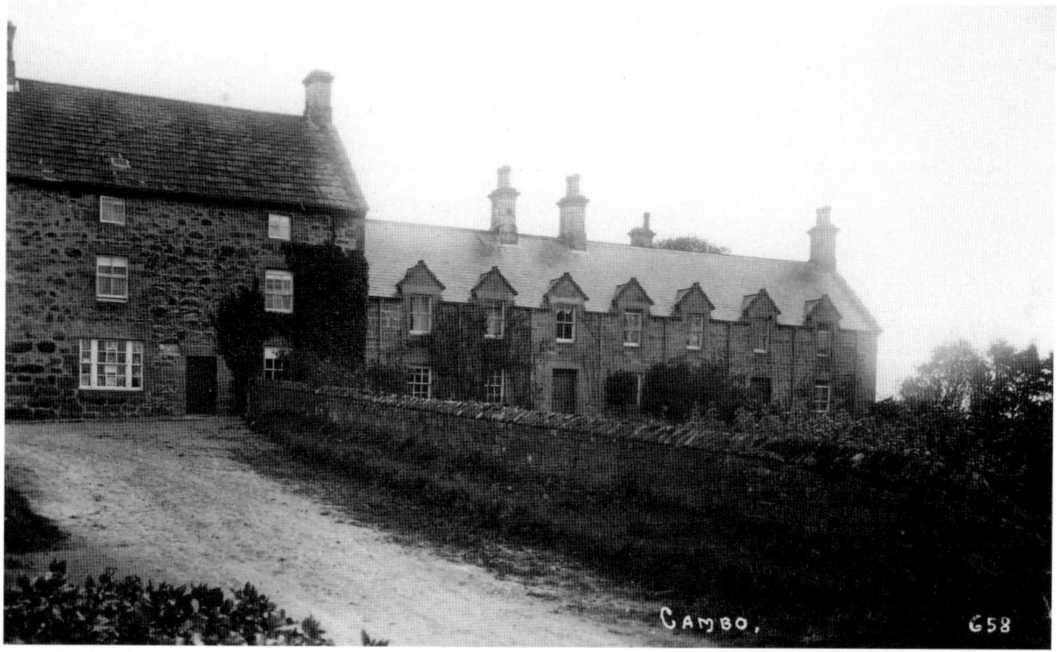


**CAMBO** The Pele Tower was the drapery and grocery shop of George Handyside (1843-1923), who was succeeded by Robert Wales (1862-1943) and his daughters. Mary (1894-1966) was a teacher and Harriet (1903-1983) ran the shop until 1952 when the Co-op took over on a 25-year lease. Norman Turbill was the manager. The shop continued with Bill and Bess Godwin (1977-1989), Bill and Dorothy Forrester (1989-2001) and Harry and Karen Herald, who came in July 2001. They kept the shop until February 2002 and the post office until February 2004. The shop became a house at the end of 2005. On the right, the Parish Room, where gas masks were stored in the Second World War, became National Trust Offices in 1958, until they moved in 1977 to the former Temperance Hotel at Scots Gap. The house on the far right was the vicarage.

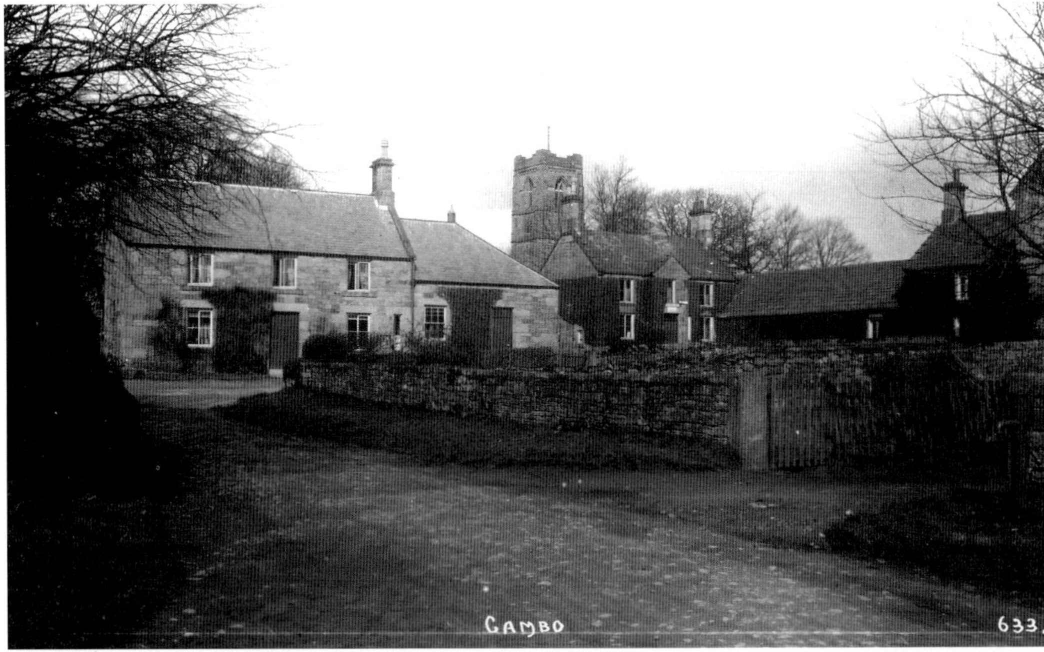


**CAMBO** Taken from Middle Row, this picture looks towards the church of the Holy Trinity, built on a low hill by Sir John Trevelyan (1761-1846) in 1842. At the end of the road, and forming the eastern end of Back Row, is the former school house and school, which Sir Charles Edward Trevelyan removed in 1885 to a new site 200 yards north of the village. The most famous pupil of the old school was Lancelot (Capability) Brown, the landscape gardener, who was born at Kirkharle in 1716. To the right, in front of the church, is East End Cottage, once the post office of Isabella Mary Hedley (1864-1932). After her death, it moved to the shop of Robert Wales in the old Pele Tower, where a George VI post-box was built into the wall. The enclosed plots in front of the village hall have become an ornamental garden and a car park.

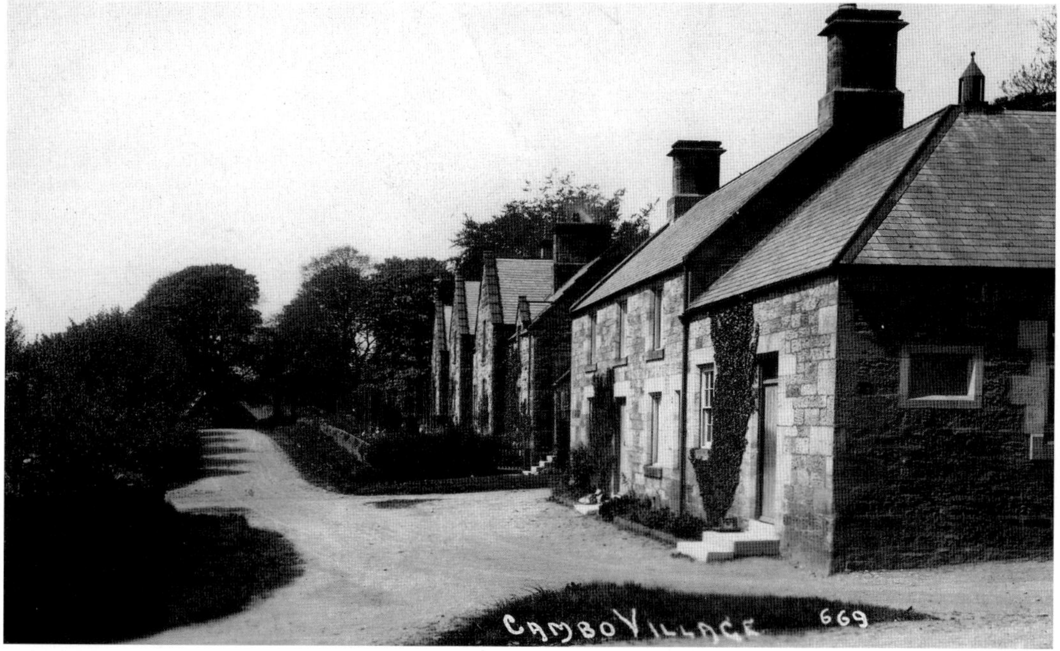


**CAMBO** This picture, taken beside the Pele Tower, rebuilt in 1818, looks west along the seven terraced cottages of Back Row towards the main road, on the opposite side of which, out of earshot of the village, was the forge of blacksmith William Wilson (1866-1951) and the shop of butcher Robert Wilson (1883-1935), whose wife Annie (1885-1964) continued the business after his death. The former school and school house are nearest to the camera. The inscription on the right records that Sir George Otto Trevelyan (1838-1928) altered and enlarged the old school house to a village hall and reading room in 1911. Just behind the wall on the left is the Dolphin fountain, built by Sir Charles Edward Trevelyan (1809-1886), who did so much to enhance Cambo during his short tenure of the Wallington Estate between 1879 and 1886.

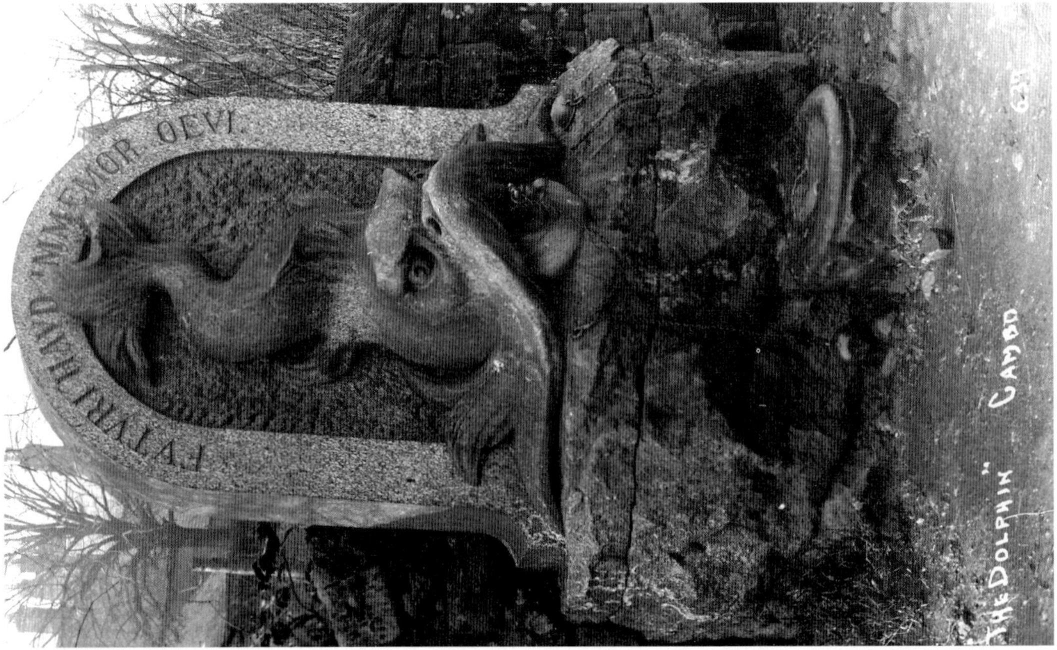


**CAMBO** Facing the former school, the Dolphin fountain was the centre point of Cambo before the arrival of piped water, though Front Row had its own supply. Water still comes from the tap and one of the two original metal cups remains. The Latin inscription, Futuri Haud Immemor Oevi, which means Not Unmindful of a Future Age, evokes the vision of two great men. Sir Charles Edward Trevelyan inherited the Wallington Estate in 1879 and spent thousands of pounds in building the Dolphin fountain, Back Row, a new school and, for the church, a fine tower, vestry, panel-work roof, memorial stained-glass windows and vicarage. Sir Charles Philips Trevelyan (1870-1958), a staunch socialist, inherited the Wallington Estate in 1928 and in October 1941 conveyed it, subject to his life interest, to the National Trust.

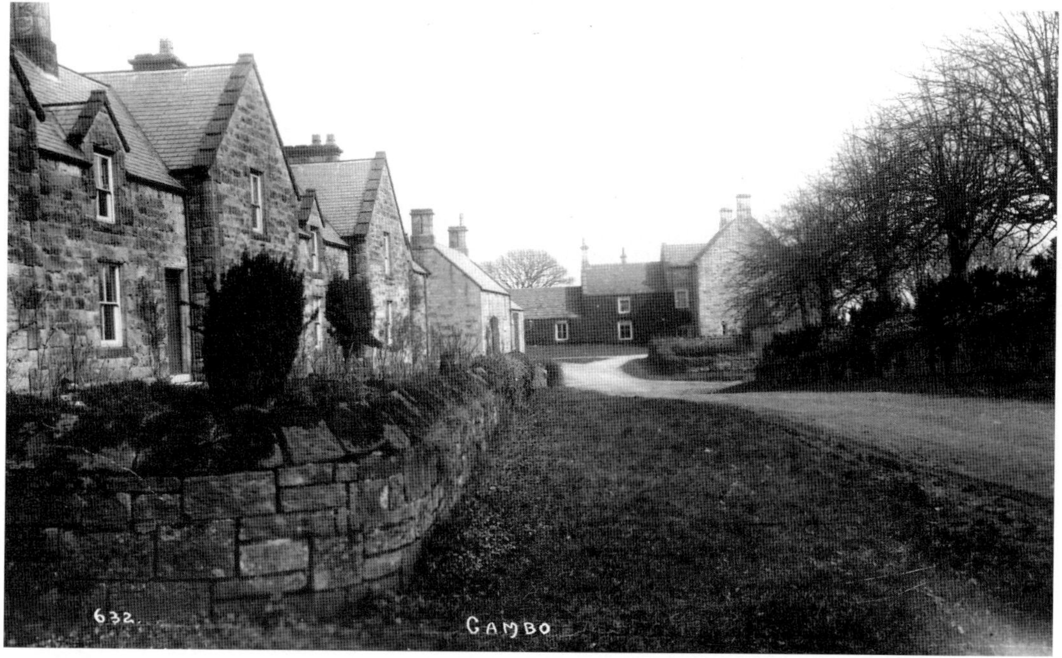


**CAMBO** Back (North) Row is a fine legacy of Sir Charles Edward Trevelyan, who also removed the old sheds and workshops from the centre of Cambo to create a village green. It was decided, however, to use this land as gardens for the seven new cottages, built in 1882, and it was over eighty years before the original scheme for a village green was fulfilled. At the end of the terrace stands the old school house, now Cambo village hall, which is still the centre of village life. An inscription records that Sir Charles Philips Trevelyan, Bart, gave the village hall to the community in 1938. To the rear of the cottages were pigsties, privies, coal houses and the communal wash-house, where, in addition to routine washing, pigs were slaughtered and stripped in the boiling water. The National Trust installed new bathrooms and toilets in 1960.

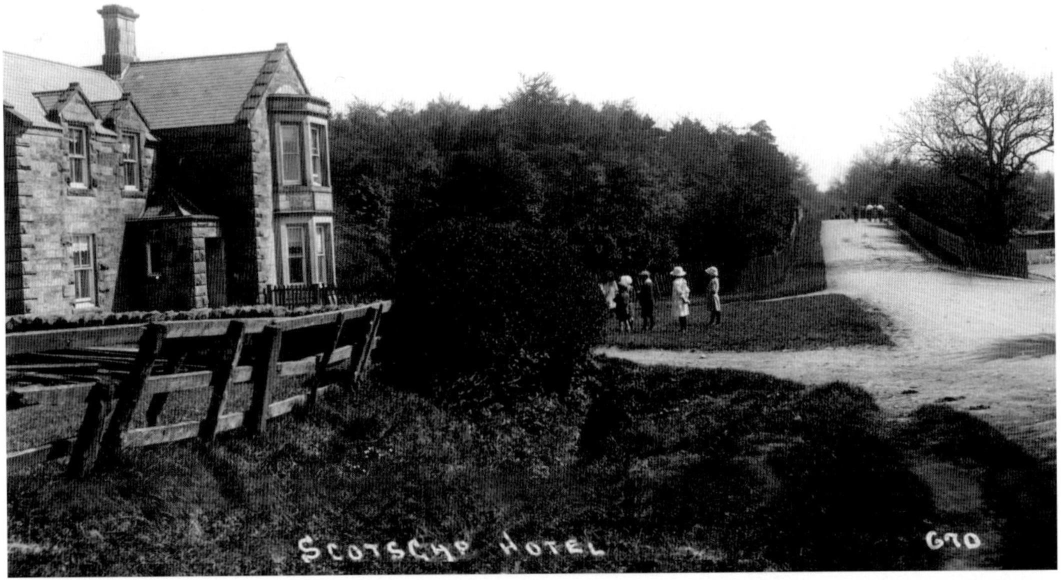


**SCOTS GAP** As part of his vision for the Wallington Estate, Sir Walter Calverley Trevelyan promoted the Wansbeck railway in the 1860s and the building of the Temperance Hotel. He was the first president of the United Kingdom Alliance, which campaigned for the total suppression of all intoxicating beverages. The hotel had a few letting rooms for commercial and agricultural agents with a trap house and stables at the rear. Much of the business at Scots Gap involved the transportation of sheep and cattle. Sir Walter Trevelyan was interested in stock-breeding and agriculture and Sir George Trevelyan had the pair of carriage horses that he hired from livery stables in London delivered by train to Scots Gap station. The days of the Temperance Hotel were numbered when the last regular passenger train left the station on 13th September 1952.

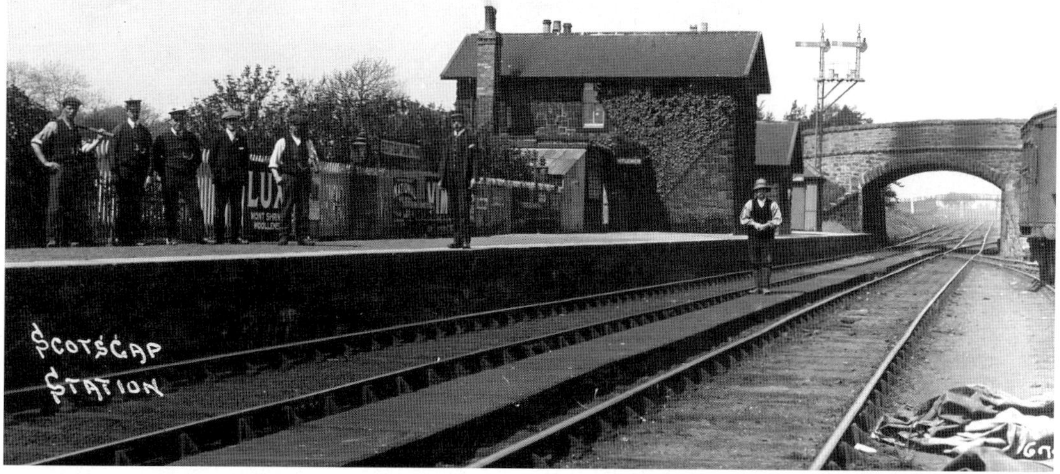


**SCOTS GAP** Joseph Robson and Tom Cowan started the agricultural business of Robson & Cowan in 1922 in a wooden shed beside the sidings on the right, behind which is Scots Gap Auction Mart. Major expansion in 1972 occupied the site of the old station, which had closed to all traffic in October 1966. Scots Gap was a railway village, promoted by two local landowners, Sir Walter Trevelyan of Wallington, two miles to the west, and Lord Armstrong of Cragside, thirteen miles to the north, both of whom found the connection with the main line at Morpeth useful for their interests in Newcastle and London. Just beyond the far bridge, now demolished, the line divided. The left track (1862-1952) carried passengers west to Reedsmouth for Bellingham and Riccarton and the right track (1870-1952) veered north to Rothbury.

**LABOUR CAMPS** were a bold experiment of the 1930s to rehabilitate the long-term unemployed. The promise of David Lloyd George that the allied victory in the Great War would produce "a land fit for heroes" was short lived. Economic depression followed the celebrations and, by the end of 1921, two million people were out of work, a figure that rose to three million over the next ten years. Industries most affected were iron and steel, shipbuilding, engineering, textiles and coal mining. The Government of Ramsay MacDonald perceived that a residue of unemployed men had lost the will to work and had become a drain on state resources. It was decided that labour camps should be established in suitable regions of the United Kingdom and be organised with the discipline of former police or army personnel. The Hexham Courant of 11th March 1933 announced that one of the first of the new Government Instructional Centres was to be opened on the former Kielder Estate, at the head of the North Tyne Valley, where 200 unemployed men would be engaged mainly on work for the Forestry Commission. Two summer camps followed at Whickhope and Byrness. Another camp opened a year later just within the English Border at Kershopefoot. Kielder and Kershopefoot were served by railway stations, with that serving Kielder, Lewiefield Halt, being especially built. Kielder eventually had around 25 staff, including three cooks. Trainees attended a 12-week course of hard manual labour and discipline. Living conditions were austere. New arrivals were issued with grey or brown corduroy trousers, a jacket and hob-nailed boots, enamel cup, knife, fork and spoon. The dining room had wooden forms and tables covered with oilcloth. Wholesome meals were handed out from an adjoining kitchen through hatches. There was a washroom and laundry with hot and cold water, a recreation room, library and sick-bay. Work began at 6 a.m. and lasted from ten to twelve hours. Tasks included digging ditches, cutting down trees and building roads. The isolation of the camps meant that it was difficult to get away in the evenings or at weekends, not that the men had much energy left anyway. Trainees received four shillings a week as pocket money and a packet of Woodbines. There were eventually 27 centres in the United Kingdom, which trained about 21,000 men a year. Their success was ambivalent and their ideology remains sensitive. The Second World War reduced unemployment at a stroke. The camps were closed and used for military training purposes or to house prisoners of war.

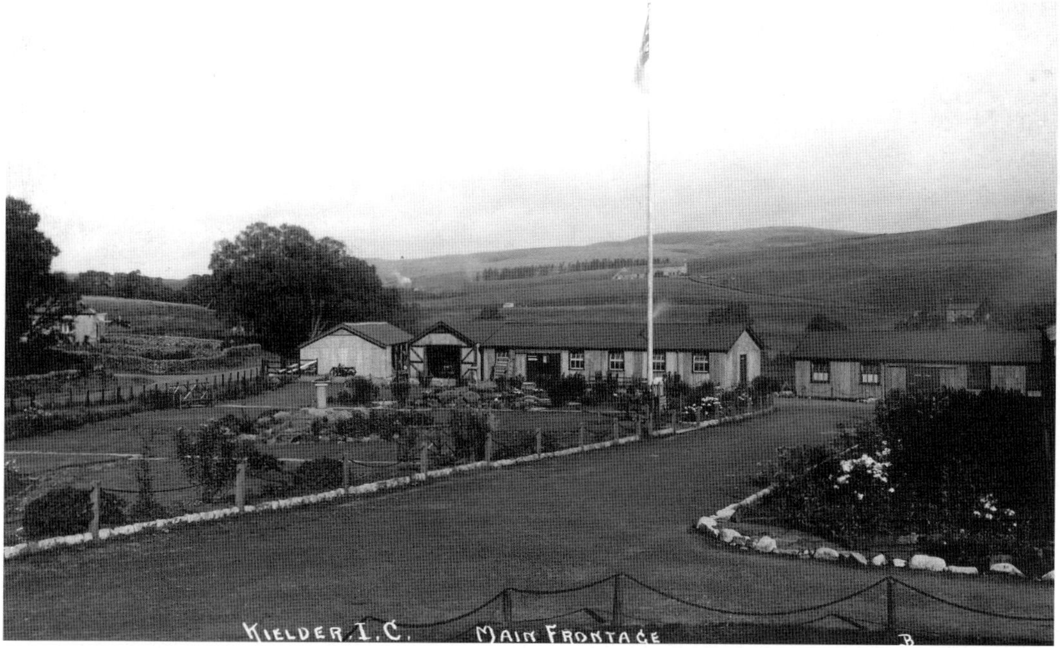


**KIELDER CAMP** The Border Counties Line runs between Kielder Camp and Gowanburn, visible behind the flag pole. On 9th March 1933, the Minister of Labour, Sir Henry Betterton, announced that a Government Instructional Centre for the long-term unemployed would be built north of the Lewis Burn on newly-acquired Forestry Commission land. Lewiefield Camp, later renamed Kielder Camp, provided 200 men with a twelve-week course of vigorous work, such as road-making, drainage and fencing. Another camp was built at Kershopefoot and summer camps followed at Whickhope and Byrness. The Second World War put Kielder to various uses. It housed Canadian lumberjacks and then injured naval personnel. It became a labour camp for Polish workers and then a Forestry Commission depot until the area was flooded in 1980.

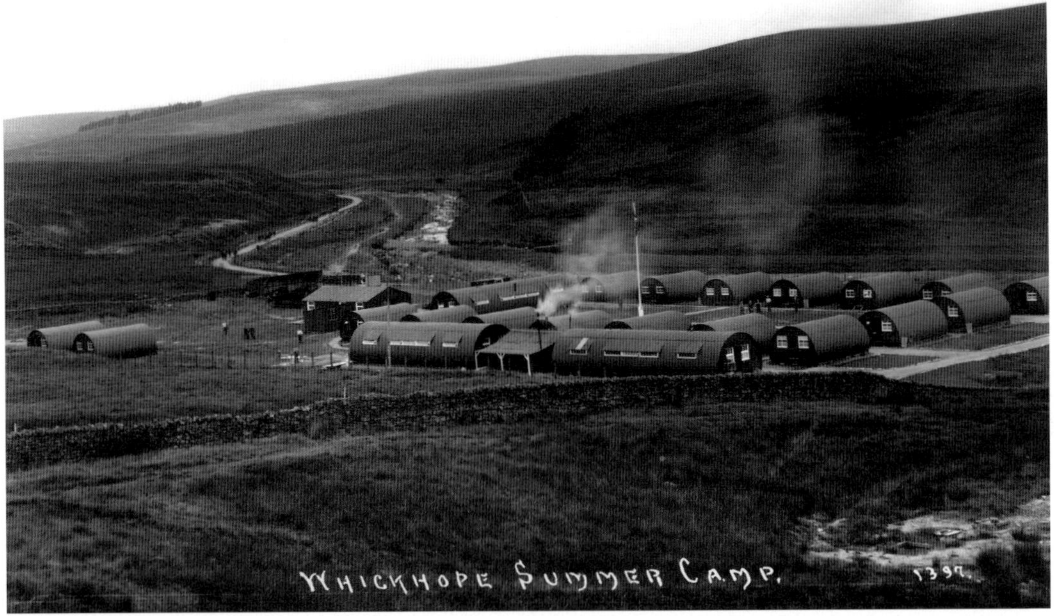


**WHICKHOPE CAMP** Leisure has now taken the place of labour, as Whickhope Camp now lies deep beneath the waters of Whickhope Anchorage. Behind the camp, the bare slopes of Bullcrag Edge have become a tree-covered peninsula, 250 metres above sea level. Visitors may now enjoy a pleasant walk beside Kielder Water, which includes part of the old North Tyne road, just south of the former Otterstone Lea farm. Groups of men, locally called Dolies, walk along the Whickhope Burn towards Low Cranecleugh, now owned by the Calvert Trust. The planting of Kielder Forest in the 1930s and the creation of Kielder Water in the 1970s have changed the landscape of the North Tyne Valley beyond recognition. Queen Elizabeth and Prince Philip officially opened the £167 million Kielder Water scheme on 26th May 1982.

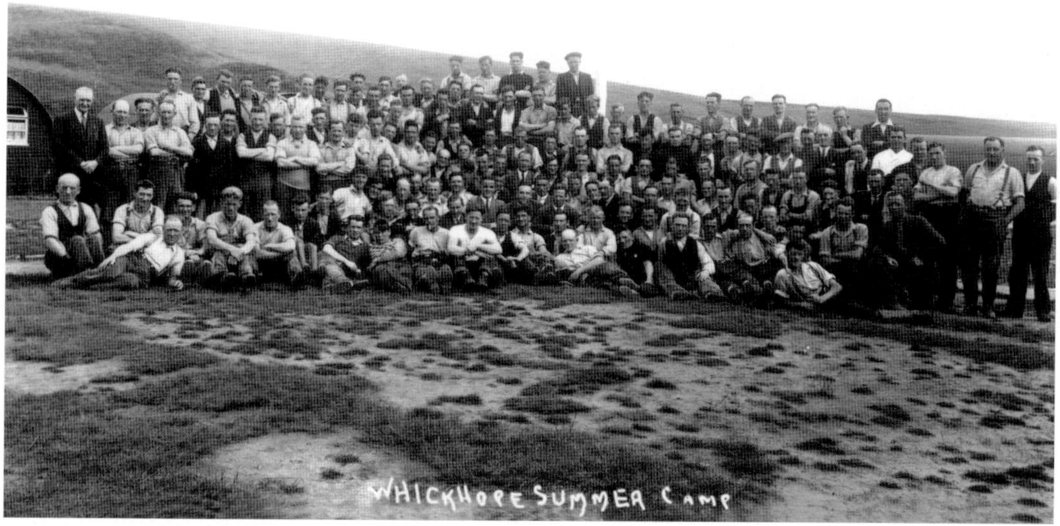


**WHICKHOPE CAMP** W. P. Collier took this picture at the flagpole probably in the summer of 1935. The 142 faces suggest that everyone is present, supervisory staff included. The trainees are wearing regulation corduroy trousers and heavy hob-nailed boots. Pictures of the men in the camps are rare. Few may have wanted a record of leaving homes and families for an isolated camp to undertake a compulsory twelve-week course of hard manual work for four shillings a week. W. P. Collier thought otherwise. As Colonel Thomas Hogarth, manager of the Kielder Government Instructional Centre, explained in the Hexham Courant of 17th February 1934, *there was unfortunately no guarantee of work for the men at the end of their three months' course but they would certainly be better fitted to take jobs by reason of the experience.*

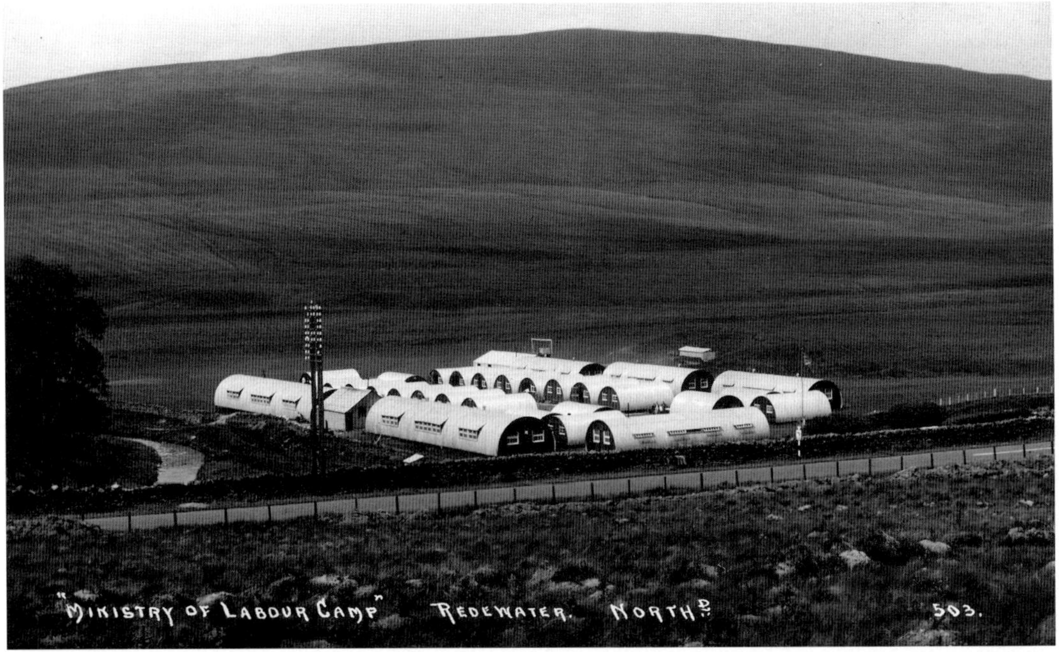


**BYRNESS CAMP** The Nissan huts had just been built when W. P. Collier propped his motorcycle against the wall to take this picture. Some ten years later, the road from Cottonshope Head and the Redesdale Ranges was built by prisoners of war to emerge opposite the telegraph pole. Situated at the confluence of the Cottonshope Burn and the River Rede, the camp looks deserted but the Union Jack flies proudly from the flagpole. The abutment of the bridge over the Cottonshope Burn is visible on the left. The bare slopes of Raw Hill are now covered by the trees of Redesdale Forest, created when the Forestry Commission bought from the heirs of Sir James Marr (1854-1932) 4,538 acres of land in 1933 and 6,879 acres in 1937. The site was sold by the Forestry Commission on 8th November 1988 and is now the Border Caravan Park.

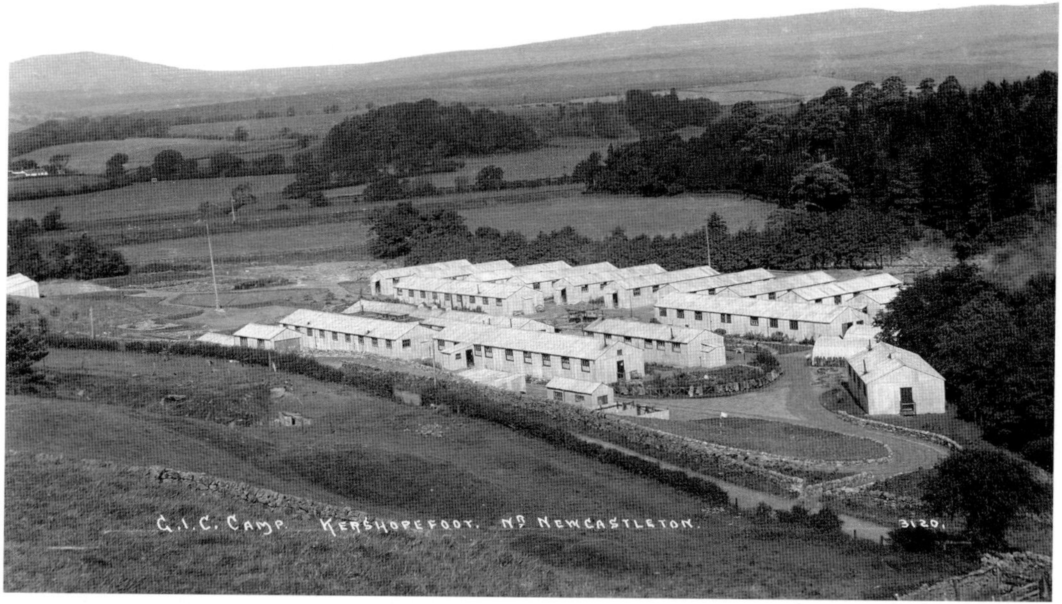


**KERSHOPEFOOT CAMP** Built at the start of 1934 as an offshoot to Kielder Camp, Kershopefoot housed 200 unemployed men on a twelve-week training course. At the start of the Second World War, foresters from Newfoundland and Canada occupied the camp and then the 49th and 52nd Royal Engineers. It was also a sergeants' training centre. After the War, it housed displaced persons, who were allowed into the cinema in the Mechanics Hall in Newcastleton, as long as they sat in the cheap seats. Ten barrack blocks, seen sideways in this picture, were built beside the Kershope Burn, which runs behind the barracks and divides England and Scotland. The long building nearest the camera housed the supervisors and to the left are the dining hall, cookhouse and mess hut. The sick-bay on the extreme right faced the entrance to the camp.

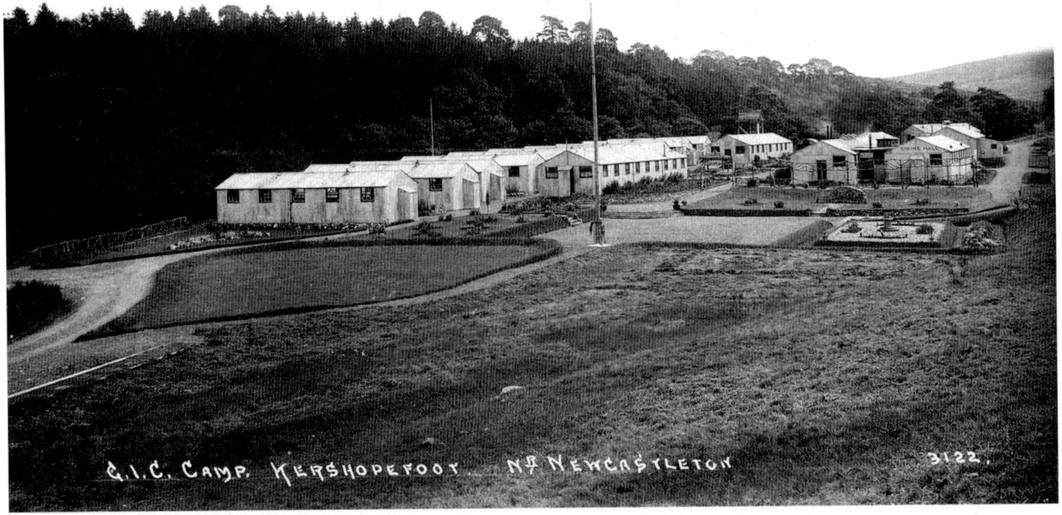


**KERSHOPEFOOT CAMP** The flagpole was the focal point of the camp, the grounds of which the unemployed men kept beautifully. The barrack blocks fringe the Kershope Burn, across which a bridge led to the recreation field. The dining hall and cookhouse are nearest the camera on the right and the mess hut is behind. After the departure of the displaced persons, Kershopefoot became a Forestry Commission residential centre, initially for female foresters. It had a cinema, canteen, shop and recreation hall, where many dances were held. Even after the Forestry Commission scaled back its operations and demolished most of the original buildings, the camp remained home to the Kershopefoot Working Men's Club. The site was sold on 1st March 1995 and the bungalow of Burnside was later built on this side of the flagpole.

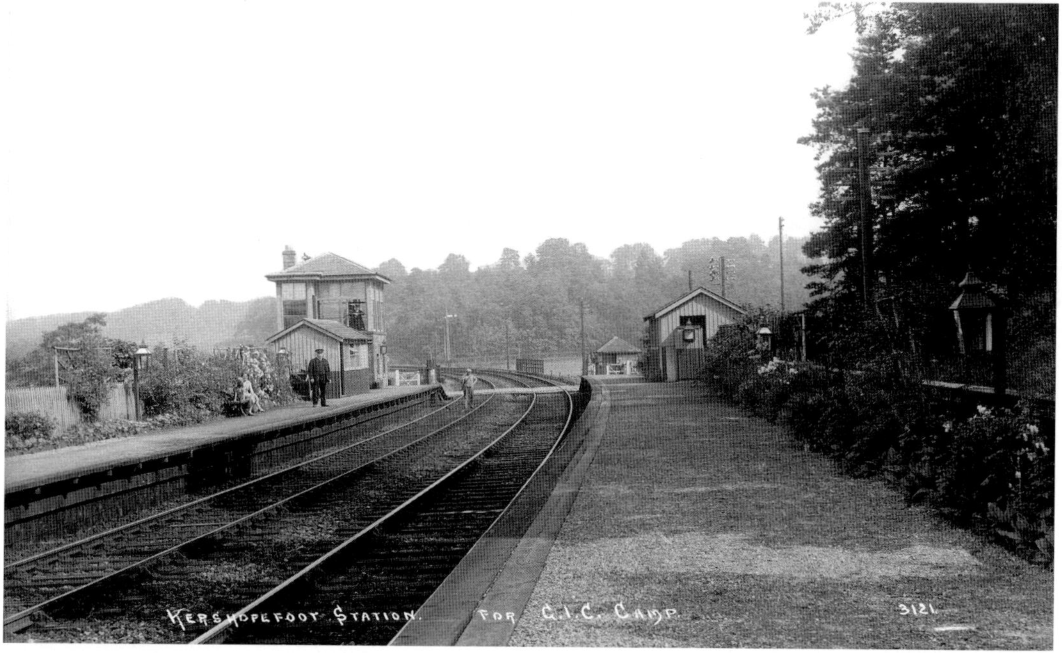


**KERSHOPEFOOT STATION** Everyone has turned out for this photograph, linesman, signalman, leading porter, who stands by the waiting room, and a young girl with her dog. As it swings north, the line crosses the Kershope Burn, which forms the Border of England and Scotland, on a three-arch bridge, visible just beyond the level crossing. The signal box on the down line replaced the earlier one on the up line after it burnt down. The period from 1934 to 1939 was perhaps the busiest time in the life of this rural station, as it was just west of Kershopefoot Camp. Nothing now remains of the station, where half a dozen trains stopped each day, except the broad track bed, which crosses the road and curves sharply towards Newcastleton, three miles away. Everything has gone, platforms, oil lamps and carefully tended plants.

**NEWCASTLETON** takes its name from the old parish of Castleton. Known locally as Copshawholm, Copshaw or simply The Holm, Newcastleton was founded on 4th March 1793 by Henry, third Duke of Buccleuch, who wished to create a hand-loom weaving centre similar to those already established for the weaving trade. Planned on a grid pattern, Newcastleton consists of one main street about half a mile long and another, not quite as long, running parallel to it, with its houses facing the River Liddel. There is a small square at each end of the main street and in the centre a larger square, intended as a market place. Many of the houses are separated from the road by broad lawns and trees, which create a sense of open space and good design. Local tradition awards the honour of completing the first house at 44 North Hermitage Street to Francis Ballantyne, who was the first to have smoke rising from his chimney. This house was demolished in 1966 to make way for the petrol pumps of the Border Autos Garage. Either William Ballantyne, said to have been the brother of Francis, or Robert Murray built the second house at 21 South Hermitage Street. Newcastleton could never compete with the weaving mills of larger Border towns, like Hawick or Langholm, and developed into the commercial centre for Liddesdale, with an incredible number of small shops and businesses, including cloggers, cobblers, tailors, drapers, a confectioner and livestock market, still in existence. Its merchants travelled the length and breadth of Liddesdale and the Borders with their wares. John Byers (1879-1968), the Bard of Liddesdale, who wrote poetry under the name of Bluebell, was born in Newcastleton and, after many travels, eventually had a small grocery shop at 14 South Hermitage Street. In his book, Liddesdale, published in 1952, he described Newcastleton as a quiet haven of rest in the very heart of a country that still retained a quota of old-world simplicity and some shreds of peace and tranquillity. *Copshawholm, or Newcastleton if you like, has not yet relinquished all its natural attractions and worthy qualities for the garish blandishments of the 20th century.* Newcastleton is an outstanding example of an 18th century planned village, which is now a pleasing and convenient centre for visitors who wish to explore Liddesdale and the Borders. Much of its rich history, especially concerning local families and the Waverley Route, can be found in the admirable Liddesdale Heritage Centre, situated in Townfoot Kirk, the old Congregational Church, at the south end of the village.

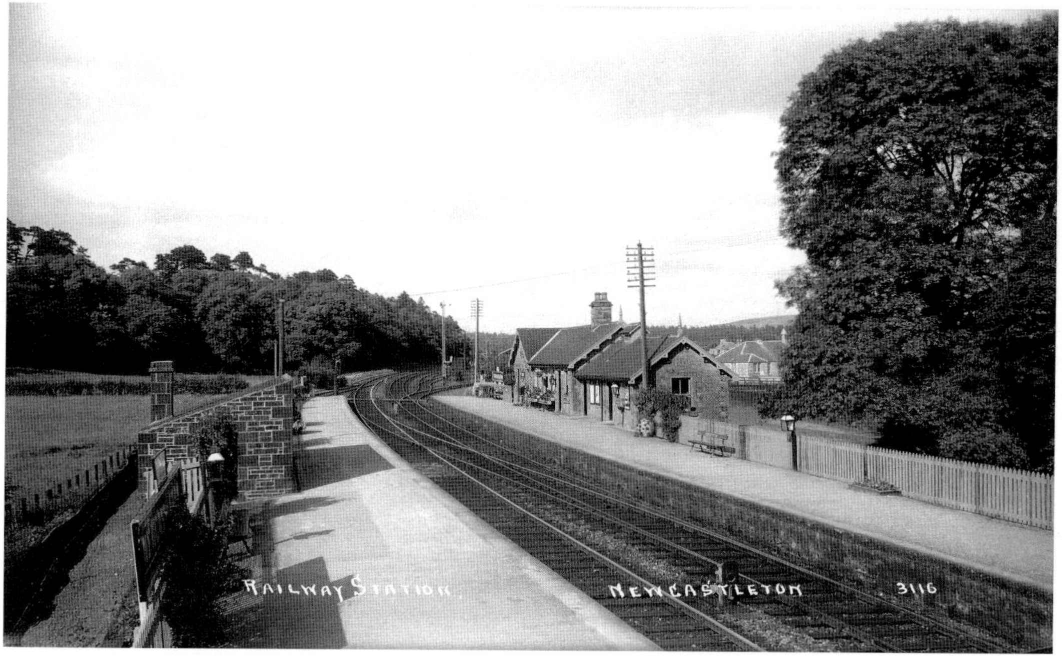


**NEWCASTLETON STATION** The Waverley Route opened fully on 1st July 1862 and ran for 98¼ miles between Edinburgh and Carlisle through rugged Border scenery. It was notorious for tight curves and steep gradients, especially between Newcastleton, Riccarton Junction and Hawick. Newcastleton made a final gesture against the closure of the Waverley Route in the early hours of Monday 6th January 1969 when 300 protestors and the Reverend Brydon Maben delayed the last train, the 2155 Sunday sleeper from Edinburgh Waverley to London St. Pancras, padlocking the gates of the level crossing and then blocking the line for 80 minutes. One of the passengers was local M.P. David Steel, who finally persuaded them to disperse, provided that Brydon Maben, who had been detained by the police, was released without charge.

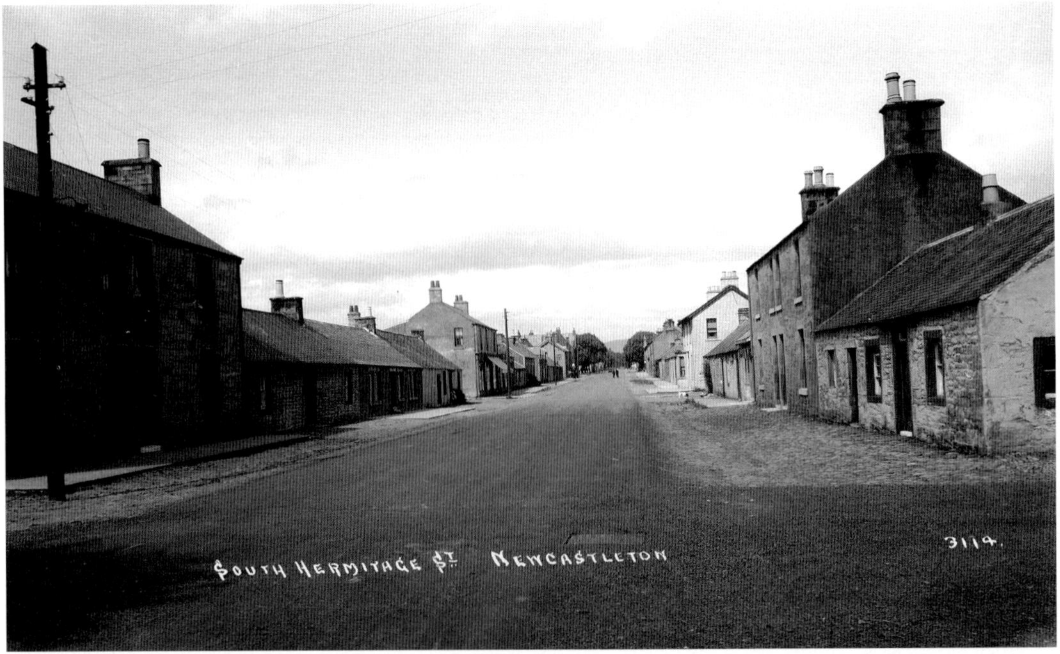


**SOUTH HERMITAGE STREET** This picture was taken north of Townfoot Kirk, the home of the Liddesdale Heritage Centre since 1994. The blinds beside the second telegraph pole shade the grocery and provisions shop of Robert Oliver (1857-1910), which his sons David, Thomas and Andrew (Dan) inherited. In 1920, Thomas and Dan bought the grocery shop at the rear of 3 Doncaster Street. David (1886-1960) continued the business, which he expanded to 37-39 South Hermitage Street, adding a drapery shop, which his sister-in-law ran, and a bakery. On the corner, nearest the camera, is 16 South Hermitage Street, the workshop of clogger William Crozier (1855-1942), who made clogs and the birch soles well into his eighties. He was the son of clogger Andrew Crozier (1826-1909) and uncle of clogger William Crozier (1896-1968).

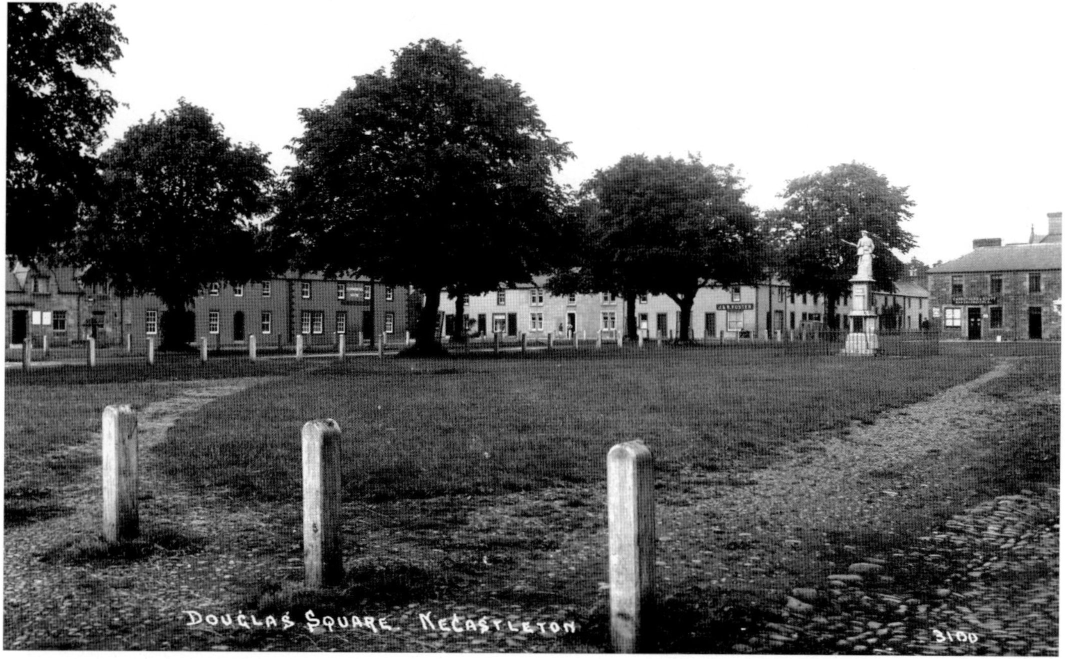


**DOUGLAS SQUARE** "To the memory of the men of Liddesdale who gave their lives for their country in the Great War 1914-1918 and whose names are inscribed here with reverence and gratitude for their noble devotion and sacrifice." The granite memorial, 16 feet 3 inches tall, was unveiled by the Duke of Buccleuch on 6th November 1920. Three bronze panels record the names of 58 local men and pictures of 46 are displayed in the Heritage Centre. Ten names were added after the Second World War and two for conflicts in Malaya and Kenya. The building on the far left was until 1958 the police station. Helen, Isabella and Eliza, three daughters of Robert Wilson (1844-1919), ran the Grapes Hotel, once sporting a wooden bunch of grapes. Frederick Guyatt ran the Commercial Hotel, called the Liddesdale Hotel after the Second World War.

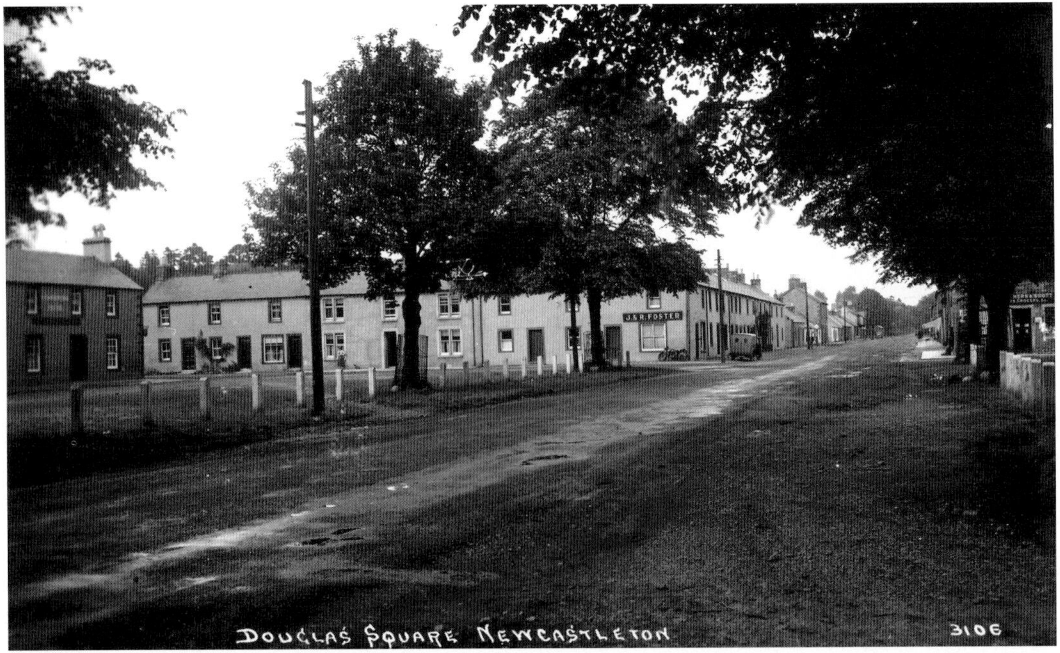


**DOUGLAS SQUARE** The drapery shop of J. and R. Foster stands on the corner and to the left is the grocery shop of Walter Edgar (1866-1933). On the right is the shop of Carruthers & Scott, Bakers, Grocers & Confectioners, who sold cakes, biscuits, chocolates, provisions, fruit and coffee until the shop was sold in 1980. A van stands outside the butcher's shop of Thomas Elliot (1883-1963), now T. Elliot & Sons and still going strong after almost 100 years. Next door was the Black Bull Inn with its creeper-covered walls. Opposite was the Mechanics Hall, which later hosted the cinema and is now the Liddesdale branch of the Royal British Legion Scotland. 3 Douglas Square housed the shop of the Davidson Brothers, Matthew, John and James, merchants, who supplied almost anything, even their own blends of tea and whisky.

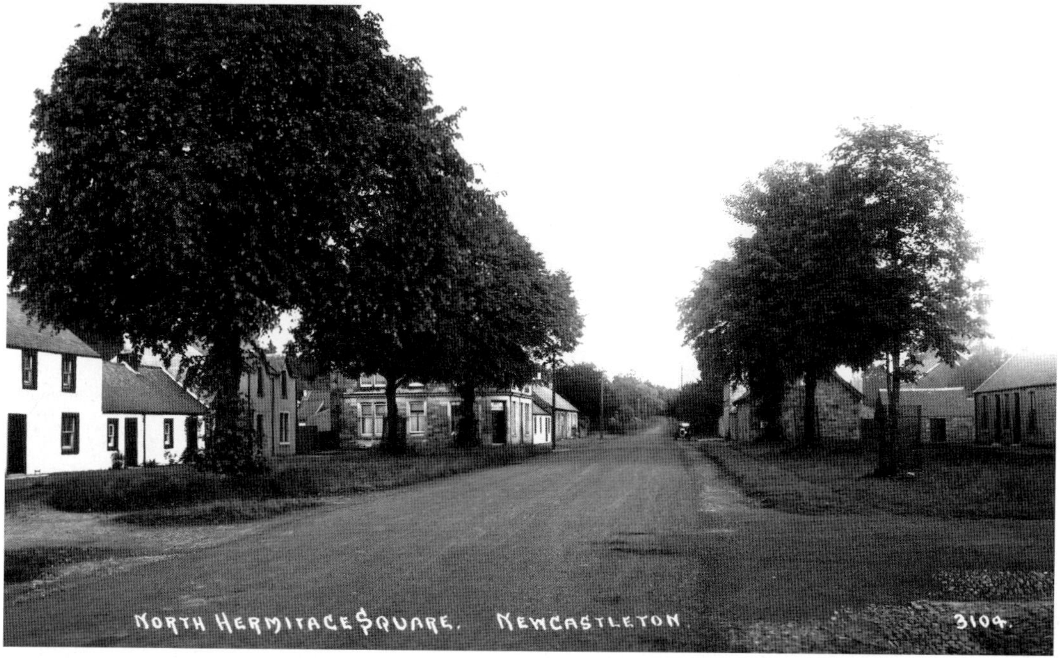


**NORTH HERMITAGE SQUARE** This Square is typical of the two squares that balance Douglas Square. Neat stone terraces face each other across grass verges that fringe the straight road through this long village. Newcastleton was built as a weaving centre but was soon overshadowed by the larger towns of Hawick and Langholm. For many years, the house on the corner, Dene House, 28 North Hermitage Street, was the confectionery shop of Janet Murray (1871-1944), who made and sold luxury chocolates. She was the eldest of the eight children of Robert Wilson, who owned the Grapes Hotel, and the widow of John Murray (1871-1904). The sweets in the window tempted children but were beyond their pockets. The shop became a ladies' hairdresser, an Electricity Board showroom and since 1957 has been a private residence.

**RICCARTON** was an isolated Border village that W. P. Collier probably visited by train, as no road access existed until the coming of the Forestry Commission in 1963. Riccarton was described as An Out and Out Railway Colony in The Railway Magazine of May 1912 and as The Loneliest Village in the Hexham Courant of 11th September 1926, which reprinted an article in The Star, London. *There has never been a motor accident in the village of Riccarton, tucked away, high above the sea, in the splendid isolation of the Cheviot Hills of Northumberland. And this is for the good reason that there are no roads. The only communication, except for a footpath across the hills to the main road, two miles away, is by railway. There are only 30 houses in this remote village. It has its being solely because it is an important junction on the Edinburgh and Carlisle main line, connecting with the LNER Railway to Hexham and Newcastle. Here you would go if you would have complete rest and peace among the mountain moors, where, on winter nights, there is a darkness and a silence that can be felt. Riccarton, among other claims to fame, has no church and, because of this, a special church train runs on every alternate Sunday to the neighbouring villages of Hawick and Newcastleton to take the good villagers to church. Tickets for it are issued free to railwaymen and their families, and at reduced fares to the other few inhabitants. The manager of the co-operative stores, the schoolmaster, for the village has a proper school for its 30 or 40 children, and the stationmaster control the affairs of Riccarton, which include two cows and a refreshment room, the latter presided over by a genial soul, who has lived in and loved Riccarton since she was a child of three. There is no cinema in Riccarton but splendid fishing may be had in the nearby rivers and streams. These are best reached by a convenient goods or passenger train, which will slow down at some pre-arranged spot and enable the angler to alight with his bicycle and cycle away. In the long winter days, Riccarton often lies deep in snow among the hills, like some Alpine village. The railway snowploughs are frequently at work to keep the track clear so that the folk may go by the church train.* Christopher (Kit) Milligan (1934-2000) was born at 18 Riccarton Junction and published his memories in 1996 in Riccarton Junction, Just a Few Lines. The Waverley Route closed on 6th January 1969 but the Waverley Route Heritage Association is rekindling something of the proud spirit that once burnt at Riccarton Junction and Whitrope Summit.

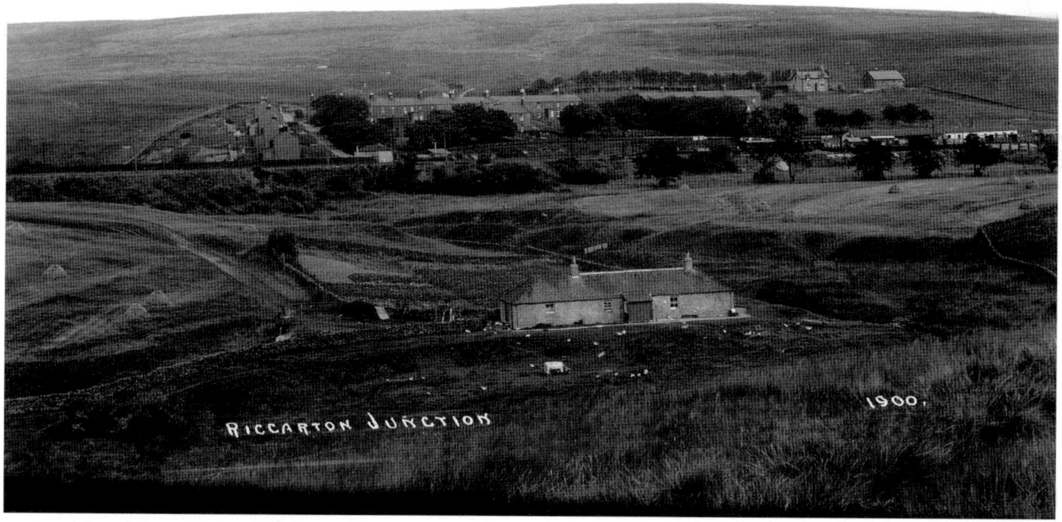


**BELL HILL** W. P. Collier has taken this panorama of Riccarton from the slopes of Bell Hill, which is 346 metres above sea level. The cottage of Leysburnfoot, locally known as The Glen, was the home of James Gray, a drainer. It was a typical two-room cottage, with a kitchen on the right, complete with large kitchen range, and living room on the left, with a smaller stove. The loft supplied additional accommodation. There were byres on the left and right. It is now maintained by the Mountain Bothies Association and called Will's Bothy after William Ramsbotham (1967-1993), an inspiring athlete, mountaineer and scholar, who died in a climbing accident. The footpath to the left of The Glen crossed the line by the North signal box and led to Phaupknowe. The old school house and single-room school still stand on the hill to the right.

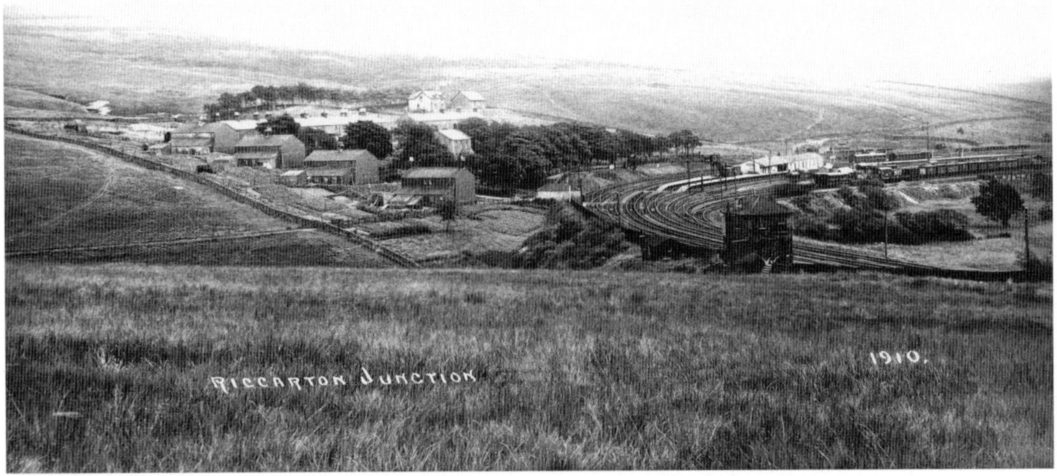


**STITCHEL HILL** W. P. Collier has climbed behind the North signal box to take this south-east view of the Waverley Route as it sweeps past the island platform of this isolated railway community, 260 metres above sea level. On the right are goods sidings, workshops, the engine shed and a couple of banking engines. On the left are two terraces of houses, the Co-op, village hall and, in the distance, the three-bedroom school house and school. Among the trees stands the detached house of the stationmaster. The distinctive stone wall in front of the four semi-detached houses (numbers 2-9) of Store Brae still remains but these houses were the first to be demolished in the mid-1960s. The North signal box controlled the sidings and the line to Whitrope Summit and the South signal box controlled the Border Counties Line to Hexham.

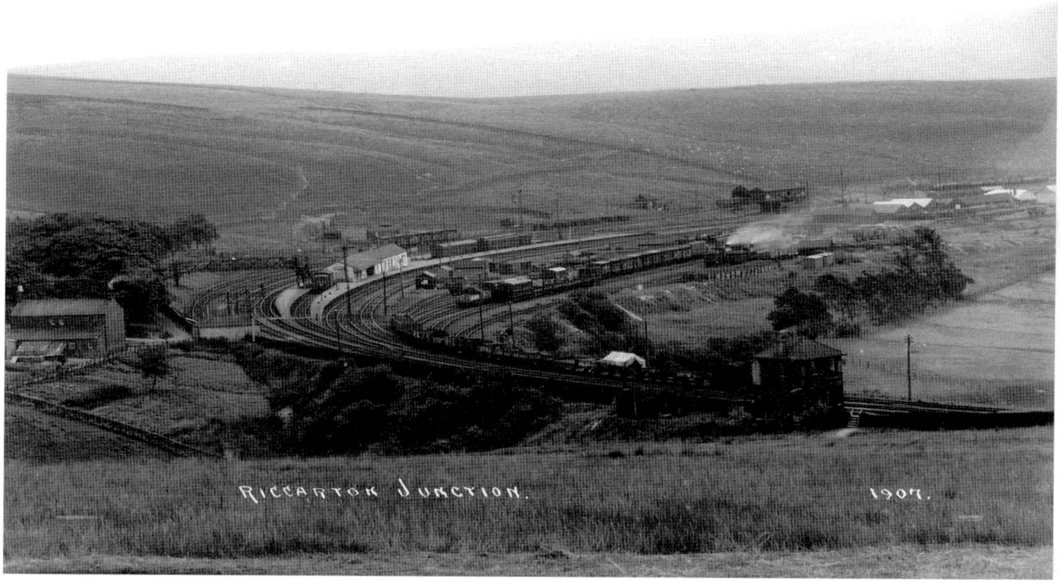


**STITCHEL HILL** At the foot of the iron railway bridge was Riccarton Refreshment room, locally known as the Refresh, which was also the village local and consisted of a public room and small kitchen with a gantry that held two barrels of beer. It had a large oak table in the middle with chairs and forms around the wall. In the south wall was a fireplace, which always had a fire burning. Opposite the fire was the bar with a teak counter and well stocked shelves, with tea, coffee, homemade scones, cakes, biscuits, sweets and alcohol. The Refreshment room closed on 28th May 1951. It later housed the Co-op, which closed in 1964 when half of the houses at Riccarton had become empty. Smoke rises from the two banking engines that assisted the heavy steam trains on the two-mile climb to Whitrope Summit, 308 metres above sea level.

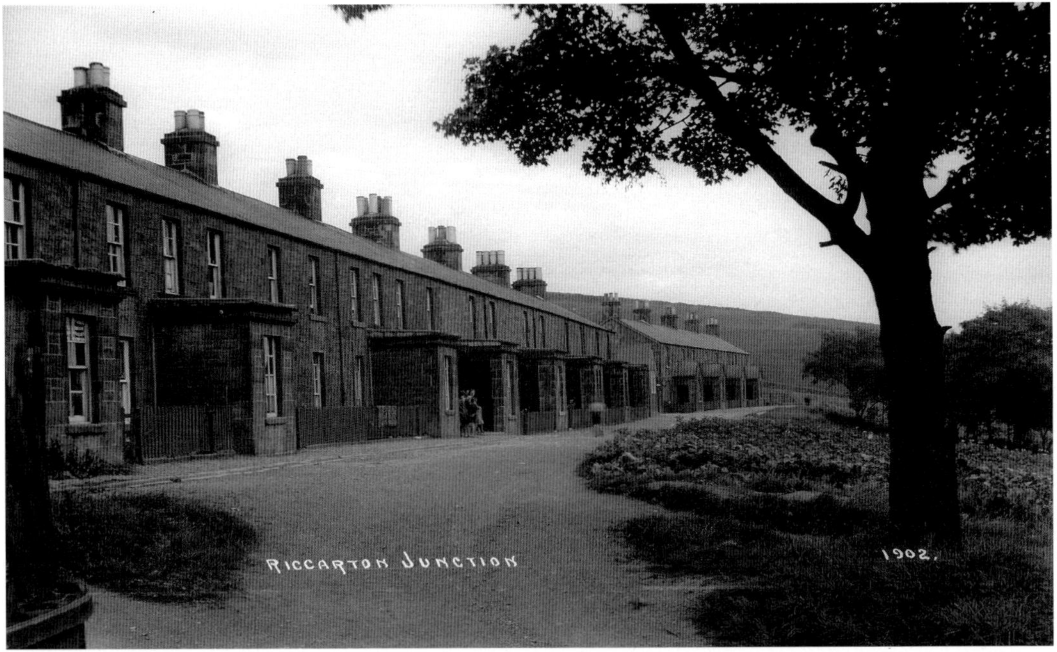


**RICCARTON** A road led up from the station past the eight semi-detached houses of Store Brae and turned right along these terraced houses and flats, which looked over neatly-kept gardens and the station platform towards Arnton Fell. The Co-op occupied number 10 on the far left until it moved down to the Under Store and then the old Refreshment room. Numbers 11-18 consisted of flats, two up and two down. Right of the vennel, where the children stand, came numbers 19-26, the last of which had the village hall built on to its side. The final eight houses, numbered 27-34, formed a separate terrace. At the end of this terrace was a gate and path to the school house and school. The whole terrace was demolished in 1967, leaving just three people in Riccarton. Nothing now remains except the tree and the shell of the stationmaster's house.

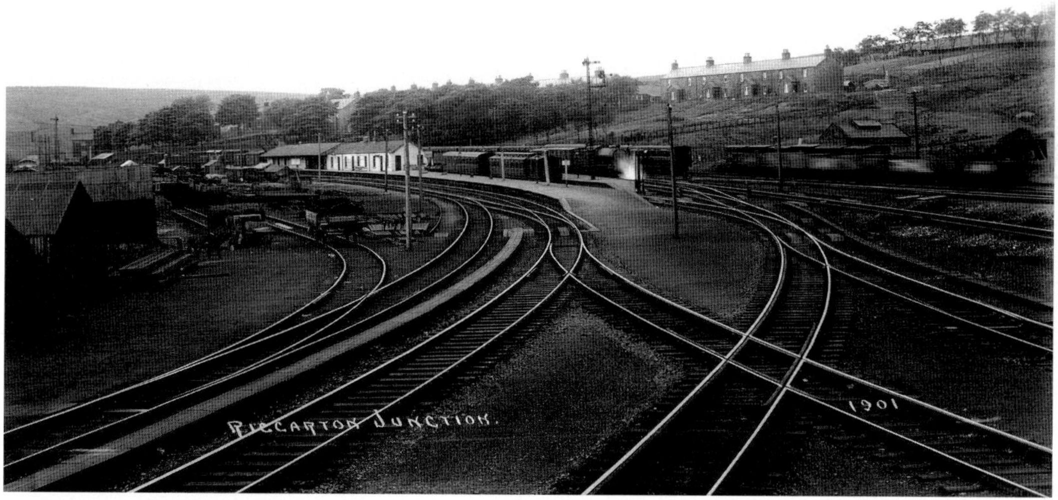


**SOUTH SIGNAL BOX** This view looks north to the watershed of Whitrope Summit and Whitrope Tunnel, 1,280 yards long. The South signal box, built of brick and faced with concrete, was at the junction of the lines from Carlisle and Hexham. For the eight miles from Newcastleton, the Waverley Route, which sweeps in from the left, has been climbing a 1 in 75 gradient. The single-track Border Counties Line comes in on the right. The Waverley Route and the Border Counties Line opened on 1st July 1862. The closure of the Border Counties Line to passengers on 13th October 1956 and the arrival of powerful diesel engines in 1959, which removed the need for banking engines, saw the beginning of the end for Riccarton. The village was dead when the Waverley Route closed despite fierce opposition on 6th January 1969.

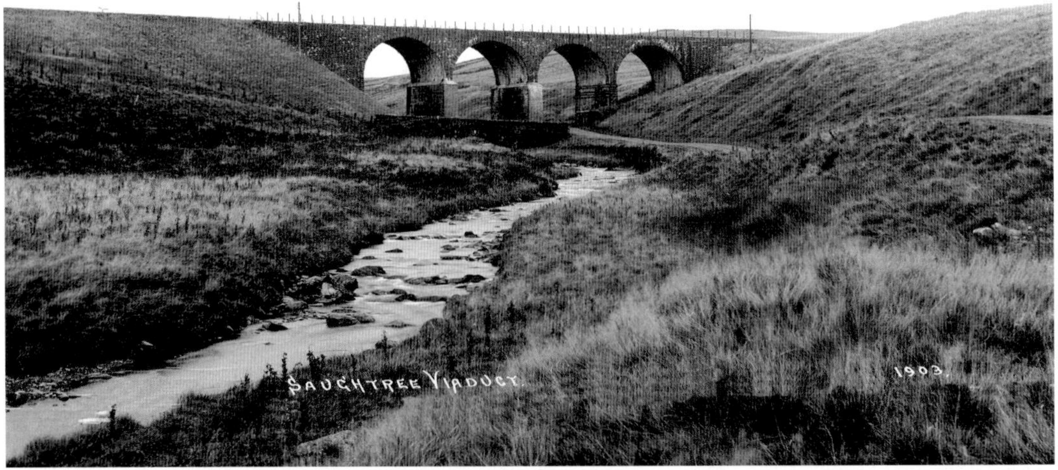


**SAUGHTREE VIADUCT** This splendid structure across the Dawston Burn dominated this bleak landscape for many years. After leaving Deadwater station on the Border of England and Scotland and climbing Saughtree Bank, which was particularly exposed and prone to snowdrifts, the Border Counties Line emerged from a short cutting on the extreme right at just over 39 miles from Hexham to cross the Dawston Burn and curve gently into Saughtree station. Demolished on Saturday 15th June 1968, nothing now remains of this fine viaduct, whose four lofty arches, each with a span of 38 feet, carried the railway 50 feet above the Dawston Burn and the road from Newcastleton to Bonchester Bridge. Each of the three main piers had additional strengthening. The small bridge in the foreground gave access to Saughtree station.

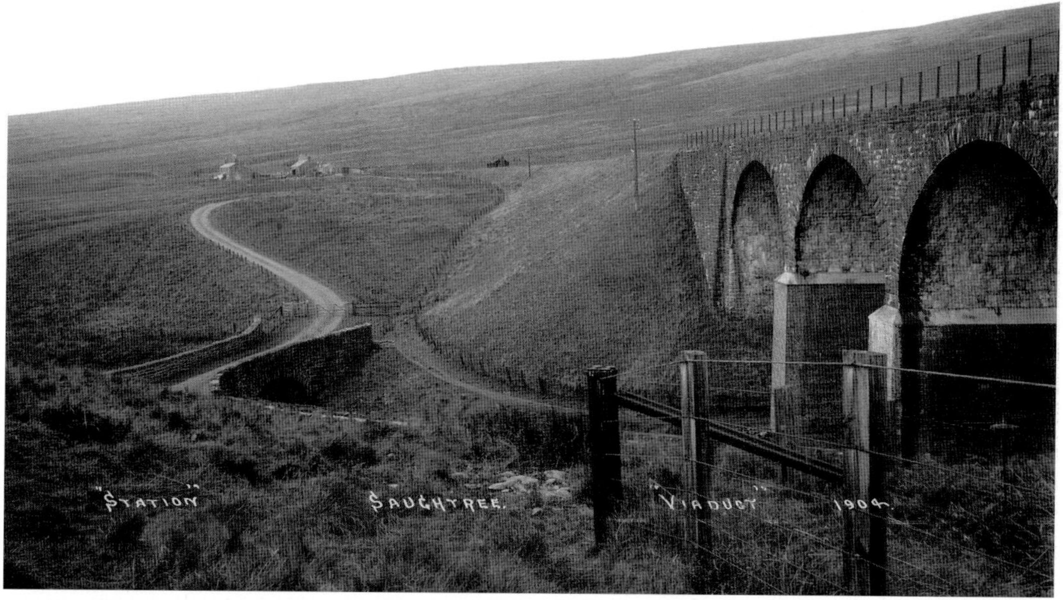


**SAUGHTREE STATION** This isolated station is dwarfed by the slopes of Saughtree Fell, along which the single track curves to Riccarton. There was one platform about 75 yards long, a house for the stationmaster, waiting room and two railway cottages. A siding faced east and had a 30-yard dock built into the bank opposite the platform. The siding was 110 yards long and ended in a further 70 yards of track with an earth buffer-stop. Wartime measures closed the station on 1st December 1944 but a limited service resumed on 23rd August 1948. Upon closure on 13th October 1956, Newcastle University leased the station as a geological study centre but from September 1987 Saughtree has been a private residence, which has been lovingly restored as a railway station with a third of a mile of track and a diesel shunting engine and wagons.

**WHITTINGHAM** inspired David Dippie Dixon to produce The Vale of Whittingham, a slender volume of 72 pages, published in 1887. His Whittingham Vale, a weighty tome of 347 pages, followed in 1895. He was the eldest son of Whittingham draper and grocer, William Dixon, by his first marriage to Jane Turnbull. Around 1862, he and his younger brother, John Turnbull Dixon, a talented artist, were sent by their father to open a second shop in Rothbury. Whittingham Vale is a collection of the local history and stories that his customers told him on his travels as a draper and grocer. The success of Whittingham Vale encouraged David Dippie Dixon to publish Upper Coquetdale in 1903. In his preface, he makes a modest request to the learned scholar and the critic *to scan the pages of "Upper Coquetdale" with kindly consideration, and to remember that it has been the leisure-hour employment of two village tradesmen.* Both volumes are full of names and places and are models of local history writing. Richard Logan (1876-1953), who wrote under the name of Glen Aln, was filled with nostalgia when he revisited the Whittingham that he had known as a boy and described his feelings in his book, Around and About Northumberland, first published in October 1943. He found that the 20th century had intruded into the village of his memories and the characters of his youth were gone: *John Rogerson, the blacksmith, is no longer there. Kit Thompson's shop, too, is only a memory; it was the shop where sometimes on a Monday morning we spent our "hap-an-nees" on our way to school. Pennies were scarce in those days when 15/- was a hind's wage for a whole week. Christopher, to give him the name everybody refused to do, was originally a cooper and always spoken of as "Kit the cooper." He was a decent fellow and allowed the big laddies to play in his shop at the back on winter nights, a bit of good social work for the lads and it kept them out of mischief.* Whittingham, like Cambo, has an old pele tower surrounded by an estate village, but unlike Cambo, which was bequeathed to the National Trust on the death of Sir Charles Philips Trevelyan in 1958, most of Whittingham was auctioned in 1927. The houses that still remain part of the Estate of the 9th Baron Ravensworth are painted green. The shops that once punctuated this vibrant village have all gone, including the court house and police station, the post office (July 2006) and the Crown Inn. With its mixture of grey slate and red pantiles, Whittingham is an idyllic village that straddles the quiet banks of the River Aln.

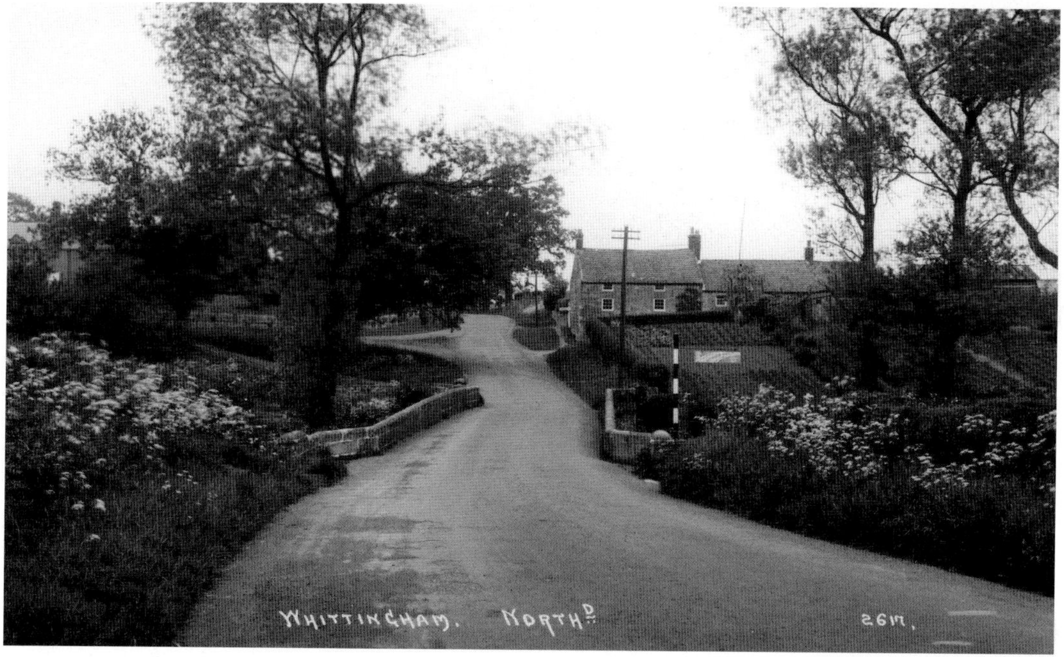


**WHITTINGHAM** The village occupies a charming site on the banks of the River Aln, by which it is divided into two parts, the connecting links being a wooden foot bridge and a stone bridge of four arches, built at the start of the 19th century, as stage coaches began to supersede pack horses. This view looks north across the stone bridge towards the Hole in the Wall, on the right, now a private residence but once a public house kept by Tom Dickinson, a local character and head gamekeeper to the Eslington Estate. Local tradition maintains that the inn, which was popular with drovers, was so called because drinks would be passed through a hole in the wall to the drovers, whose condition might make them unwelcome visitors inside. The Castle Inn was a posting house, where coaches would stop for refreshments and a change of horses.

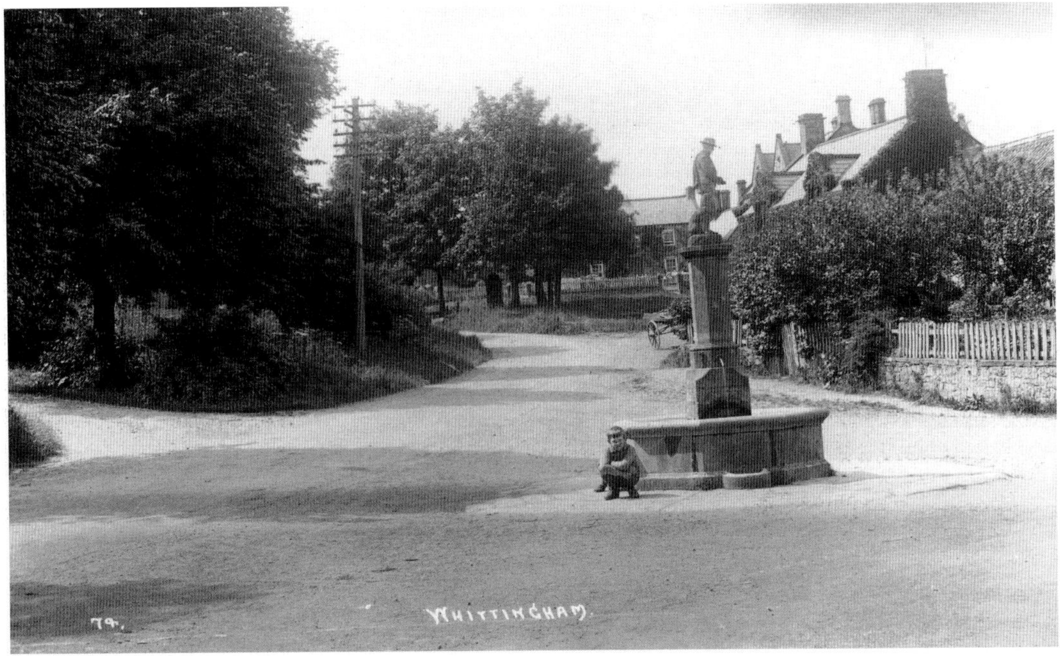


**WHITTINGHAM** The Ravensworth Memorial was erected in 1904 on the sudden death of Athole Charles John Liddell (1833-1904), 3rd Earl of Ravensworth, by his wife Caroline. This fountain and the pant on the village green, built by the Right Honourable Henry Thomas Liddell, 2nd Baron Ravensworth in 1865, are reminders that Whittingham was once part of the Eslington Estate, 2,863 acres of which were put into 73 lots and offered to tenants, who bought almost half of the lots, before the rest was auctioned on 22nd April 1927: *twelve valuable grass farms, with Substantial Houses and Premises, also virtually The Whole of the Village of Whittingham, comprising Small Houses, Business Premises, The Post Office, School, School House and Thirty Cottages, also the Fully Licensed Bridge of Aln Hotel and The Castle Inn.*

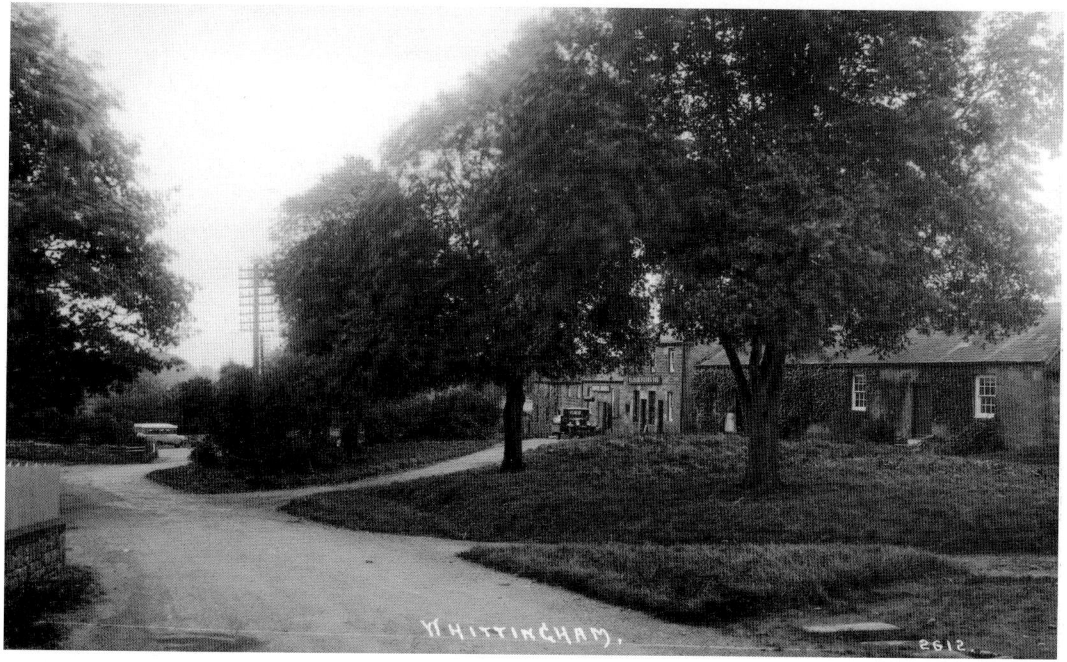


**WHITTINGHAM** A lorry stands outside the extended grocery and general shop of William Dixon & Son, which William Dixon (1812-1878) established in 1839. The shop remained in the Dixon family through his son William Dixon (1852-1927) and his grandson Henry Dixon (1892-1966), who sold the business on his retirement in 1955 to Arthur and Ruby Greenhalgh. The shop continued for another 25 years under several owners but finally closed and became a private house. William Dixon opened another shop in Rothbury in 1862, managed by his two sons David Dippie Dixon (1842-1929) and John Turnbull Dixon (1844-1926). David used the knowledge that he gained from his travels to produce two books, Whittingham Vale (1895) and Upper Coquetdale (1903). John was an accomplished artist and illustrated both works.

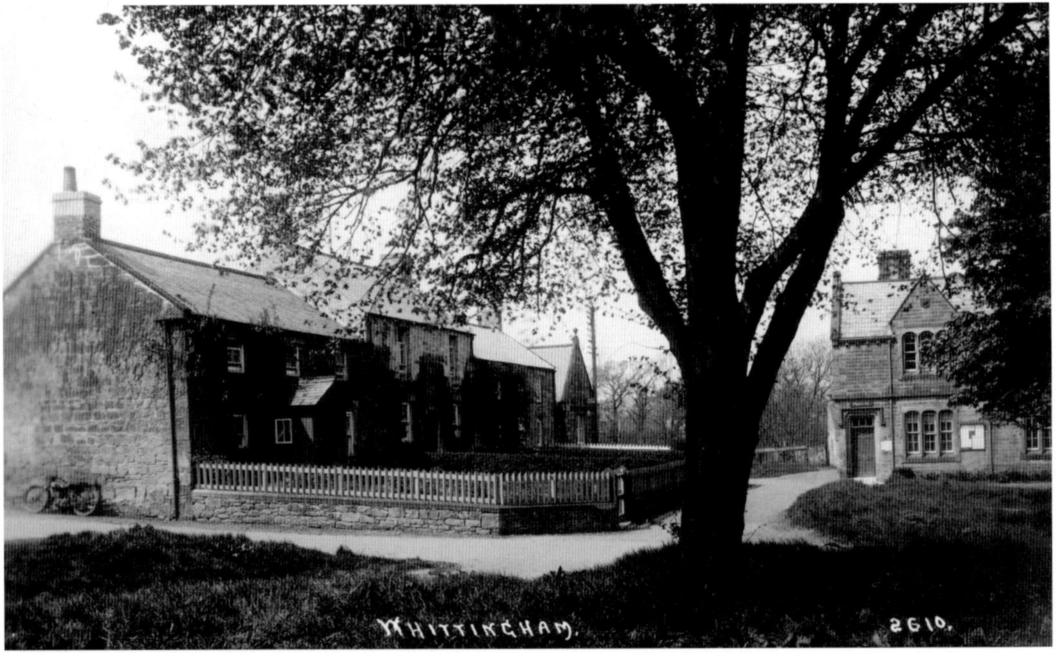


**WHITTINGHAM** Standing his motorcycle against a wall, W. P. Collier has taken this view of Garden Terrace near the butcher shop of Walter Scott (1837-1894) that his son Robert (1863-1957) ran after the death of his father. Beyond the furthest of the three cottages was the post office that Octavia Lane (1874-1951), fourth daughter of Luke and Jane Henderson, ran until her death. Built in 1859 on the site of the Mason's Arms, the fine building on the right was the court house and police station. The police station and cells were on the ground floor and the magistrates sat upstairs. The police station closed in 1978 and for fifteen years was used as the Northumbria Police Expedition Centre for police cadets and deprived young people. After standing empty for several years, the building became a private house in March 1997.

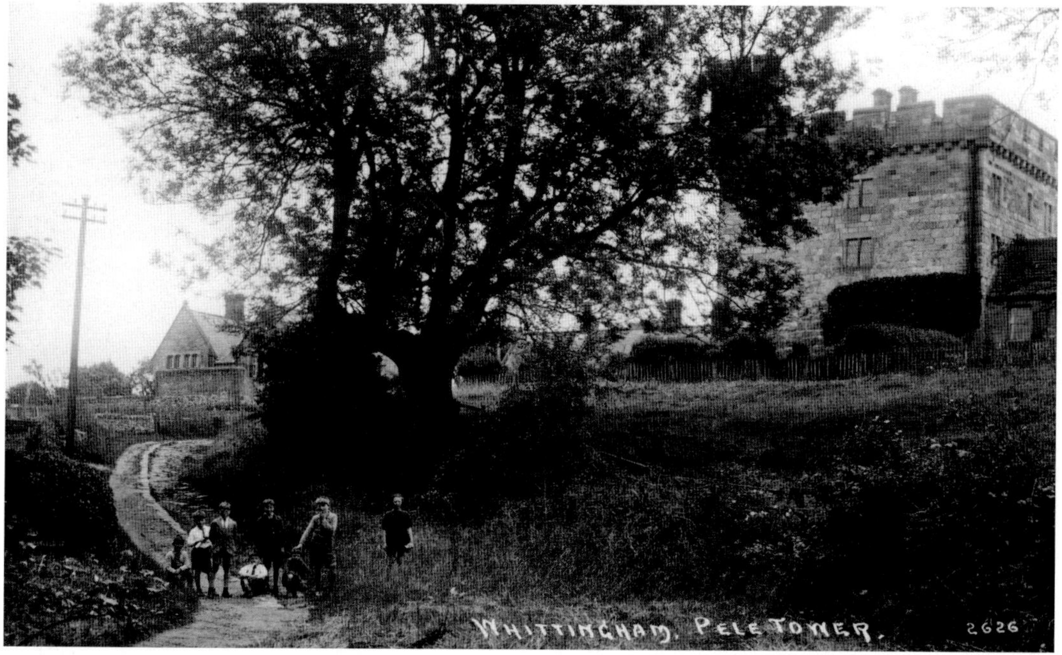


**WHITTINGHAM** To the right of the children rise the solid walls of Whittingham Tower, a 14th century pele, which stands on a steep hill overlooking the River Aln, as it flows gently through a grove of beech trees. Lady Isabella Ravensworth (1801-1856) converted the tower into almshouses for four single people or married couples, who received an allowance from the Ravensworth Estate. *By the munificence and piety of Lady Ravensworth, this ancient tower, which was formerly used by the villagers as a place of refuge in times of rapine and insecurity, was repaired and otherwise embellished for the use and benefit of the deserving poor. A.D. 1845*. The Tower was used as almshouses for over 120 years but, after standing empty for many years, was put up for sale in 2003 and has since been restored as a private residence.

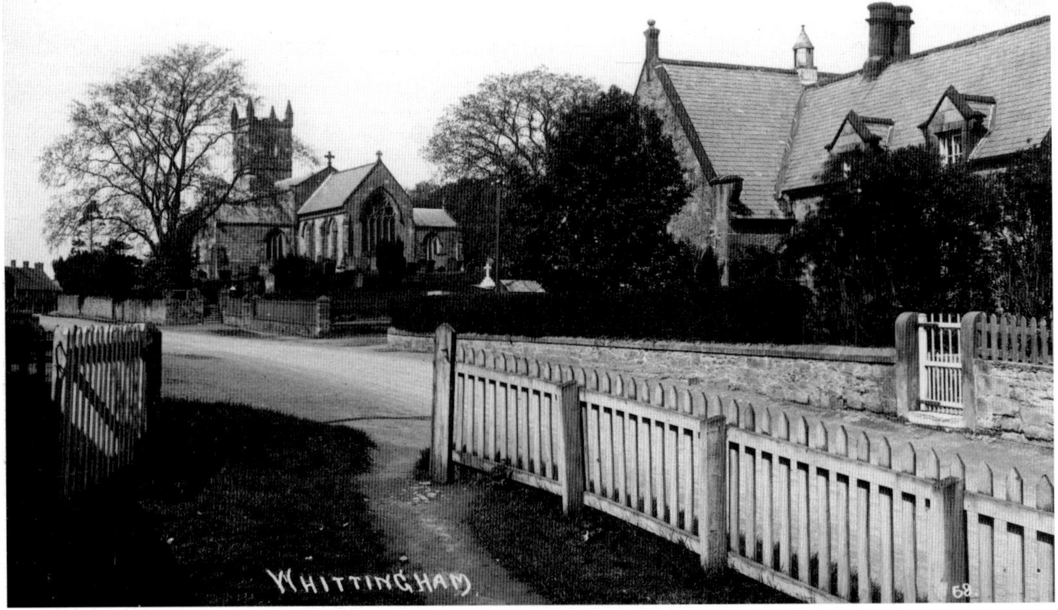


**WHITTINGHAM** W. P. Collier has crossed the River Aln by the wooden bridge to emerge on the North side, often called Church Town, which has the Whittingham Memorial Institute, built in 1924, and the church of St. Bartholomew. In 1840, the architect John Green was asked to replace the upper part of the Anglo-Saxon tower with a more conspicuous Gothic version. In 1968, a modern school was opened behind the old school, seen on the right, and school house, which are now private houses. The South side was the commercial half with the post office, police station and court house, butcher, cobbler and shop of William Dixon, opposite which was the smithy of John Rogerson (1835-1907) and shop of former cooper Christopher Thompson (1821-1898), who gave David Dippie Dixon so much information about Whittingham.